# THE PERSON YOU CAN BE

ROY A. BURKHART

# THE PERSON YOU CAN BE

HARPER & ROW, PUBLISHERS · NEW YORK, EVANSTON, AND LONDON

*TO ALL THOSE WHO HAVE BEEN
MY SPIRITUAL TEACHERS
AND
TO THE MANY WHO HAVE BEEN COMPANIONS
IN THE QUEST FOR A FULLER LIFE.*

# CONTENTS

# PREFACE

One of the unique opportunities I found in the spiritual laboratory where I worked for a quarter of a century was to try to
bring the resources of sociology, psychology and psychiatry and
a warm and dynamic theology of religion into a working and
meaningful relationship.

These pages are not theory. They describe much that was
learned as persons grew toward wholeness from birth and as
those who got into bonds sought to move into whole persons.
You will find, too, much that is autobiographical in these pages.

My deep gratitude goes to those who gave me permission to
use quoted material. I am deeply grateful, also, *to all those who
graciously gave me permission to use experiences from counseling and other pastoral work. Permission has been received from
all but those who are deceased.*

I am indebted to many physicians and psychiatrists in Columbus, Ohio; to Drs. Singer and Morgan of Chicago, under
whom I had a controlled clinical training; to Anton Boisen, who
was one of the first to open my eyes; to Drs. Franz Alexander
and Karl Menninger, to whom I owe a great debt; to the people of First Community Church, and the past and present staff
members; to my son, with whom I have had the privilege of
working, and who, as a physician and close confidant, has meant
more than he knows, for he is a keen man in healing; to my
daughter-in-law, for the beauty of her person and for her life
as a wife and mother; to my daughter, who, during a polio sei-
zure, practiced what I preached, and whose wholeness and
womanhood make her a "radar star" to more people than she
realizes; to her husband, Paul Selby, Jr., who has been one of
the greatest counselors I've ever known and an abiding friend;
to Henry Pfenning, who for twenty years has led a personal
growth group in the laboratory where I worked; to Group Seventeen, whose persistent research has been a great personal inspira-

tion; to the members of First Community Church for giving me a lifetime contract with the support of love and money to provide the freedom to work; to Otis Maxfield, who now stands where I once stood and works where I once had the chance to do research with a great people; to Gerald Heard and Paul Brunton, my chief teachers in the life of prayer; to F. W. H. Meyers, who, in Newcastle, Pennsylvania, jarred me to the center of my being; to the editorial staff of Harper & Row, who did much to make my feeble words speak with more meaning; to Rosemary Weimer, my personal secretary, who for a quarter of a century has been helpful, creative and wise, with a wisdom born out of prayer and unfailing loyalty; to Mrs. William C. Ailes, whose secretarial skill, loving faithfulness, and enthusiasm never flagged no matter how many times pages had to be redone; and to Hazel Burkhart, my wife, who has been joined with me on the path that leads to being and doing for more than forty-three years.

ROY A. BURKHART

*By the Gulf of Mexico, writing as I look out*
*to where water and sky meet. Easter, 1962.*

# INTRODUCTION

This is an hour in history in which man can no longer avoid giving thought to how he lives, for the world has never been in such peril. Man is in a crisis out of which he does not know how to negotiate himself. Despite his urgent desire to live, he is making fantastic preparations to end his life in this dimension.

The peril is greatly intensified by the fact that man, who has discovered the secret of such amazing mastery of nature, has not had time to acquire a like mastery of his own creative powers. Often at this point in time he seems actually unable to act rationally or even decently.

The hope for our world lies in the possibility that man can achieve in his own personal life this mastery he has won over nature. After all, the bomb which can blow up the world has no language, no mind, no means of communication. It is man who has a language that is intelligible, who can speak with other men—not as a beast or lunatic but as the greatest in all God's creation.

Here and there we see people who do achieve mastery in their lives. They find mastery in friendship and in human relations which calls forth the best in each person. They have freed the inner light that flickers in all men, allowing it to illuminate their own lives and those they touch. They have freed themselves from outer tyranny. They are responsive and aware.

If they marry they also find mastery in their love, as a husband or wife and as a parent. They find mastery in their vocational life, in their church life as children of God, and as citizens in the community and nation.

On the other hand, there are those who find mastery only in one area. They may achieve physical health and, to a degree, mental health; but they fail to make a success of their marriage

or vocational life. Or a person can be outstanding in his vocational life but sacrifice his health and have a heart attack or
nervous breakdown at the age of thirty-five or forty. Or it is possible for one to be a "good fellow," to have a comfortable home
and to be successful in his vocational life and yet to make no
contribution to his church or to the life of his community. Or
one may find mastery as a person, a friend, a lover, a parent, a
worker, a churchman or citizen. An individual's moral awareness may guide him to give leadership to the various causes and
voluntary agencies in the community but ignore the nation and
the world. Such a man is completely "local." He depends entirely on others to determine the destiny of mankind. He is pro-
community but (by default) anti-world, anti-humanity.

Man's inner mastery must become his primary concern. He is
in a race for space yet is unsure of who he is. Instead of loving
himself for the person he can be, he is riddled with self-hate.
Man is a rope stretched from the beast to the superman; one
more tug and the rope will break. This happened in the Second
World War, when Hitler tugged, and we saw a nation of technological cannibals.

We are today conducting vast research on nearly every aspect
of life except on the nature of man. We are spending billions
on technological research in order to achieve greater mastery
over nature, while only pennies are allocated to problems of
human nature and human relations. Man can no longer delay
finding out who he is, why he is, where he is headed. Answers
to these questions are basic if he is to build peace by consent
rather than coercion, and to fashion a civilization in terms of
world community rather than a giant state.

"What is man?" is a key question whether we ask it in wonder,
as did the Psalmist, or in bafflement as did Job.

Alexis Carrel stated the dilemma of modern man clearly:
"Modern civilization finds itself in a difficult position because
it does not suit us. It has been erected without any knowledge
of our real nature. It was born from the whims of scientific discoveries, from the appetites of men, their illusions, their theories

and their desires. Although constructed by efforts, it is not adjusted to our size or shape."

Why has man's knowledge outdistanced his wisdom? Why has he mastered nature and brought himself, on the one hand, to the dawn of a golden age and, on the other hand, to the brink of nuclear suicide?

Could it be that the last area of research is himself? Is it not easier to do research outside of himself? It is interesting that man discovered America before he discovered the circulation of the blood.

Perhaps the answer has to do with the conflict in man. As an ancient poet said, there is both dust and divinity in man. There is a part of him that seeks to build a hut in the swampy lowlands, and another that would seek to build a cathedral in the verdant hills. Instinct says, "You are meant for the earth"; aspiration cries, "You are meant for climbing." Goethe caught the spirit of this paradox in the first part of Faust:

> Two souls are housed within my breast,
> and each alas will wrestle for the mastery there.

Goethe contrasts the urge to "hug(s) the world where sweet the senses rage" with the higher spiritual longing which leaves "the murk for lofty heritages."

This brings us to the point of this book and to you the reader. You are the only creature of God who possesses awareness. And, unlike all the rest of living creatures, you are unspecialized. To you has been given an amazing gift—the freedom to become. No matter how far you go or what excellence you attain, you will never achieve your fullest potential. But you can go far. You can find mastery; you can grow beyond mediocrity toward excellence; you, in a great measure, can fulfill your highest destiny.

Each person in his best moments seeks to work toward the realization of his fullest potential. No one wants to fail. In fact, I believe that the psychotic, the sociopath, the neurotic, the laggard, the loafer, the dependent—every one who fails—is trying to come through, trying to get from where he is. I have met those who said, "I don't care"; I've worked with some who gave in to the desire for death; but even with these there was evidence that the negative view on the conscious level was not in accord with the view held by the deeper self. When a person moves toward fulfillment, he feels right with life. When he moves into deeper bondage, he knows pain.

People prize life. Think of the great number of institutions of healing and the great army of those dedicated to restoring life. Think of the extent of the drug business, the demand for books, the institutions of learning. We're in a psychological revolution; all over the world there is a desire to live, a passion to taste life to the full, to make the most of life. Never have so many people been so aware of their problems; never have so many sought help. Every counselor and counseling agency is overloaded. Never before, in my own experience, have I sensed such hunger for answers, such eagerness to move from problems to solutions, as I find today. On the surface some persons may seem not to care; they may appear to be self-satisfied, caught in the routine and satisfied with life as it is. But when they find the stimulus of a creative group, when the social situation awakens them, they become hungry to know. They have a desire to become. They become aware that the real inspiration in life is not in routine but in experiment. And I have found this to be true not only of youth, but of men and women of all ages in all walks of life. I met with a group of young business executives and their wives, for example. When the group awakening took place, the members would not conclude until after midnight. There has been a follow-up with a number of them ever since.

On a number of occasions in the last three years I've met with groups which I got talking. Often they became so stirred they refused to stop for a coffee break. This has been particularly true of youth groups. Recently I spent five days in a community where I spoke with fifty high school young people each evening. At the end of the week many of them said good-by again and again. "Why are you saying good-by so often?" I asked. "We never felt so alive," came the answer. "We never wanted to know like this; we never before felt we were persons. We have become alive and don't want to lose it."

This is the spirit of people when awakened. But it is important for us to see that if we're to keep going, we need fellowship; for man is now developed to the point where he can go forward only in fellowship. Some mistakenly believe that they can become "the person they can be" on their own; others feel that God in His infinite grace will do it for them. Both are wrong. No person can become whole without God, nor can he become whole by God's activity alone. I have discovered that I cannot have a garden without God; God has chosen not to have one without me, but together we can have a great garden. The amazing fact is that when we have God's infinite gift and our complete response, the impossible becomes possible. Limitations that have been imposed or that we have accepted become cancelable.

We now come to the real issue: the person you can be, you are now becoming. What is the nature of that person? Is he growing in mastery or does he have a need to master or is he a victim?

If this person you are becoming is growing in mastery, he is coming to know who he is. This is the prime requisite, but we will see that this person can only know who he is by knowing the One to Whom he belongs. This relates to one of the most serious aspects of the human condition—the identity crisis. There are those who trace man back to an ape; there are others who trace him to God. Is he a clod or a broken wing? Much of the feeling that man is just a clod grows out of popular expositions of the teachings of Freud, Darwin and Marx, out of which have come such assertions as the following: man is an animal; the struggle for existence and natural selection have determined the nature of the human animal; as he grew in the awareness of himself and his fellow man, social institutions fulfilled his wants and gave him his convictions and his standards of values; his consciousness is not that of a unified, whole person, but a hunger with a psychic nature determined in part by society and in part by the variety of influences to which the organism has been exposed.

All of this means that for man life has little meaning. The scientific method, which enabled him to perform miracles, has at the same time left him without a sense of his own uniqueness. He is an animal.

Man's opinion of himself has been affected also by the relaxation of moral sensitivity. Some people consider moral values to be nothing more than traditional structures built by men of another time. These persons are saying in effect: "There can't be any divine will in all of this. If moral standards arise out of ageless customs, I don't feel that I'm obligated to abide by them. I shall originate customs for myself."

In answer to this, is it not important to consider that God may be speaking His will through customs evolving through the centuries? These people want a precipitate God. He must speak a world into existence. He must declare in a moment all the laws of life or He is no God at all.

In all generations the great masters of spiritual research have felt that in every time and place God is working with the infinite patience of an artist. They feel that, as we plant a seed and in time have a growing garden, so the Eternal One has planted in the subsoil of human life germs of everlasting truth that gradually come to flower.

The masters feel that God speaks to men through custom. They mean the fundamental customs on which society is built, those evoked through ages of painful movement of the race, customs drenched with the blood of souls. And undergirding our customs is the force of conscience. It is native, original, elemental. It is far more likely that conscience is the basis of social values than that it is the product of social values. To be sure, people give different content to the categories of right and wrong. "But," they ask, "what invests right with rightness and wrong with wrongness?" The answer is native to the soul. It is the far, faint whisper of the voice of God and the universal moral authority with which He speaks.

As we go through these pages, we will consider deep inner motives to understand not only where man came from, but why he goes in the direction that points to his maximum fulfillment. Whatever the background for man's low estimate of himself, his loss of identity is a very real factor in the human condition. The insights of Riesman and Fromm have indicated this fact as did Kierkegaard when he said, "The greatest danger, that of losing one's own self, may pass off as if it were nothing; every other loss—an arm, a leg, five dollars, a wife—is sure to be noticed."

Thomas Kelly, in his *Testament of Devotion,* says that modern man is a committee of selves who outvote each other. F. Scott Fitzgerald describes the different persons he saw in himself and then concludes, "So there was not an 'I' anymore—not a basis on which I could organize my self-respect, save my limited capacity for toil that I seemed to possess no more. It was strange to be no self, to be like a little boy left alone in a big house, who knew that now he could do anything he wanted to do but found there was nothing he wanted to do."[1]

Dr. Robert J. Lifton's book, *Thought Reform and the Psychology of Totalism,* gives a penetrating analysis of how China became a communist state and claims that it was due to an "identity crisis." The book gives a sharp warning to America.[2]

We will see that there is only one true solution to this identity crisis: a person must be born again, as Jesus said a long time ago. This is basic if he is to become a person who fulfills his true destiny. We will see that of all God's creation man alone is not driven by built-in forces which compel him to develop in a certain way. He has from the beginning tunneled up from the dark and damp because he heard the clang of the tools of the Master Workman above. He has always been drawn by a dream of the future of yet unachieved excellence; and he does not fulfill himself through what others have done alone, though this is always helpful, but through the power of the spirit, through the power of God in life, which ever calls to the person he is. Man grows not only through the use of the insights of science but through the use of the insights that come with surrender. He grows not only through observation but through communion. He grows not only through what happens in the laboratory but through what happens in the sanctuary.

Douglas Steere put it beautifully when he said that the resources for the fulfillment of the self are where they always have been: "Not downstream among vast levees and deltas of programs and plans and administrative structures, but far upstream where all religious renewal comes from: in the quiet places of the hearts of men, in the solitary conversations of consecrated men and consecratable souls confronting the mighty acts of God which, by the way, are still going on."[3]

Let us further consider this person you are becoming. To what extent is he free from the bondage of the past so that he can be creative in his interdependence and interpersonal relations, and to what degree is he wholesomely independent? This question is related to a second aspect in the human condition. Prevalent today is an increasing dependency. Our mental institutions are filled; every therapist and counseling agency have long waiting lists. There are thousands of persons not sick enough to be hospitalized but whose neurotic behavior makes other persons sick. Something goes wrong; millions of persons fail to grow beyond dependency; they are in such bondage to the past that they are unable to think of themselves without shame or without the need of adoration from others. This can be observed not only in the vast numbers of psychopaths, neurotics and psychotics, but also in the tendency on the part of young people to seek security rather than opportunity.

Another thought about this person you are becoming: is he free to love and be loved? If so, then wholeness will grow around him; if not, then sickness will increase. I have never dealt with a sick or troubled person where the one identifiable factor wasn't that somebody forgot to love him.

This relates to another factor in the human condition: a famine of tenderness and gentleness. To be free to love and be loved is a spiritual achievement. Often, what is thought to be love is either strategy to get one's way with another person, or to possess and be possessed. Love is the total response of a whole person to another person; it is the capacity to see the person as he can be; it is, moreover, the expression and revelation of the real self to another person without any thought of return. Elemental love is understanding. If you become a whole person, you can love everyone though you may not feel affection for all persons. The absence of this freedom to love is the real cause of most mental and much physical illness. When love is withheld, sickness grows; when it is freely given, persons become whole.

As a result of the lack of this freedom to love there is an absence of tenderness and gentleness. Halford Luccock once said, "People rub elbows with many but hearts cry out to be understood."

It is reported that in one research laboratory a girl was hired to pet white mice, for with this practice the little animals respond better to experiments.

Going another step, to what is this person you are becoming devoted? What is his supreme devotion? Is it worthy of the devotion of all mankind? This, too, is related to another aspect of the human condition—a confusion of goals. So many persons are preoccupied with getting. This in itself is all right. Jesus said, "Ask and you shall receive." However, the individual must concern himself with acquiring not only possessions but wholeness.

The tragedy results from the next step. Most persons keep, and this is spiritual suicide. To get is good; the next step is to dedicate what is acquired as well as the means of getting. But the ultimate dedication of the person himself to those goals which are worthy of the devotion of all men is of prime importance. There are today two ways of life abroad in the world. One is based on coercion and compulsion and operates within a small group of people, members of the Communist Party, working through men and women who do not know who they are. The other way of life is based on consent and compassion and operates on the amazing and thrilling idea that God works through men and women who know who they are. So to become a person is the ultimate goal. To get, to dedicate, then to become a whole person through which the purpose of creation can be fulfilled—this is a worthy goal, and when one is truly devoted to such a goal and free to fulfill it, he can meet the requirements for enlarging and extending our way of life with its democratic ideal.

Finally, is this person you are becoming a leader? What is a leader? Is he one who fosters the conditions in which leaders can grow? Is he one who helps people achieve a team spirit? One of the desperate factors in the human condition is a famine of leadership, leaders who are sensitive enough to go forward with the very wisdom that runs the universe.

Having asked you searching questions about the person you are becoming, let me say that these pages describe the difficult paths that I personally have traveled. As I share with others, I often feel lonely, for I was once where they are. While I have moved from problems to solutions in many areas of living, still I write in the spirit not only of one who is ready to share fully with you, but of one who is in the deepest sense a fellow searcher.

I was a high school principal for three years, superintendent one year, in national youth leadership eleven years and minister of a church, where for twenty-five years I saw people develop in wholeness and persons in bondage become whole, growing wonderfully into their highest destiny. For three years I have been working with groups in the church, with schools, seminaries and universities and in seminars of business and professional groups. My doctorate at the University of Chicago was not in a technical field but rather in the field of real human relations: I made a study of the social adjustment problems of senior high school people.

No one can solve your problem. I cannot do so, nor would I want to do so. I respect you too much to try. You are a person with unlimited resources. The most I can do is to travel with you the paths that lead to the destiny that is yours, for the person you can be, as we have said, you are now becoming.

As we share together you will discover that Part I outlines the points of beginning. Part II describes the unfailing resources. Part III gives directions along the roads of destiny. Part IV interprets the whole-making relationships which the person you are becoming will develop in terms of your true destiny. The final chapter outlines a way to evaluate progress.

# PART I. THE POINT OF BEGINNING

## CHAPTER 1. GUIDING PRINCIPLES

We are now ready to move from where you are. There is no other starting place—not where someone else is, not where others think you are, not where you'd like to be, but where you are. Any other point of beginning could be a false start.

Before we discover the point of beginning for the person who seeks to grow from bondage into wholeness, there are some guiding principles which others have found to be helpful.

### THE FIRST PRINCIPLE: *We Must Proceed on Faith*

We do not start on the basis of what we know; we begin in terms of faith, but we need to understand the meaning of faith. Faith is not wishful thinking; it is reason grown courageous. Faith is not an act that by-passes reason. Look where you will and you find that faith is a dominant factor in the fabric and tissue of life. Without faith no enterprise would or could be undertaken. Uncle Sam did not *know* he could split the atom, but he had reason to believe he could. Then his reason became courageous. By gambling two billion dollars, his reason and faith became knowledge.

Faith that the summer sun will follow spring rains leads the gardener to plant his seed in the moist, brown earth. Experience brings him to this act, but he has the faith that his has been a trustworthy experience that will be repeated again.

We have every reason to have faith. After all, there aren't

1

many airplane collisions; there aren't many automobile wrecks. There are more than there should be, but there aren't many. If such disasters were not exceptional, all insurance companies would go broke. Instead, they flourish, which means that the universe is trustworthy.[1]

By faith men build their bridges, lift their skyscrapers, and send their ships into uncharted seas. They have the faith that the stars will remain in their courses, that the laws of stress and strain will be constant; they have faith in the continued cohesion of steel and concrete. By faith, men stake their lives on a belief in God; and that belief does not fail them anymore than summer fails to follow spring or the law of gravitation fails to operate, or a perfect chord of music fails to be harmonious.

Yes, life is built on reasons that reason cannot *know*. Take a human cell, a microscopic speck of living matter—what is it? A whirlwind of billions of electrons, orbiting many million times in a fraction of a second. The nerve cells of the brain alone measure millions to an inch. Yet look at all of them and you will not see the mind. How does the cell become the man? How does the man become conscious of himself? It is strange that people withhold faith in God because He's a mystery.

Mystery is all about us; and that is why we say life is built on reasons that reason cannot *know*. Faith is at the heart of life. Challenges lie at the heart of life because we go further on faith than on certainty. The research doctor does not know, save by the glow of the mind, that he can find a cure; the uncertainty lures him on and gives his quest nobility. The mountain climber does not know if the unscaled mountain can be conquered—the distant peak draws him like a magnet.

Jesus knew, by some deep surmise of the soul, that a strategy of love would win. Others had opposed hate with hate and force with force. Suppose He met hate with friendship, force of body with the strength of the spirit, killing with sacrificial love! The unknown beckoned Him and He answered in faith that to Him was knowledge. He embarked on a wider ocean than did Columbus. The unknown that puts faith at life's center is always the spur in medicine, in building a better world, in the crusade of redeeming love, in suffering made victorious.

We can be thankful for the mystery that makes us build all life on faith, that calls us to reverence if not to worship. Can a scientist with eye glued to the microscope, watch a cell without experiencing emotions akin to awe? This cell is not the movement of a machine; it is the primal fact of life. Can the astronomer watch the sky without a sense of reverence? Someone has said, "An irreverent astronomer is mad." Can anyone watch the miracle of health without being subdued and moved? Can anyone hear great music without being cleansed? Can anyone see Jesus crucified—His body broken but His love unbroken despite the venom of man's perversity—without being pierced with humility? Even if the great unknown does not lead us to worship—to put out our hand to touch God's face—it will bring us to silence.[2]

The unknown that puts faith in the heart of us not only gives life its incentive and leads us to reverence, it also brings renewal of the soul. When we go beyond reason, we find renewal. Faith is higher than reason. Why halt your car to look at a panorama of red oaks? To do so may make you late, but your soul will have a chance to breathe. There is nothing in the books of logic to justify our allowing the faint, tremulous note of a violin or a crushed, faded letter to bring back a flood of tender and beautiful memories. But memories as well as hopes have the power to bless. There is no good reason why the remembered touch of a baby's hand on our cheek, or the moment when we walked along a trail with a great soul, should make us strong in the face of temptation, but some of us know that it can. It is not reasonable to fall upon our knees and lift our soul to God Whose existence we cannot prove; but since the dawn of time men and women have been doing it, and since the dawn of time, they have been rising from their knees calmed, with floodgates of inner courage mysteriously broken wide open within them.

So our first principle is that we proceed on faith, which is reason grown courageous. But even more significantly, faith is seeing clearly—with the illumination of the One to Whom we belong.

## THE SECOND PRINCIPLE: *Man Alone Is Aware*

A second principle has to do with man's conception of himself. One of our troubles today is that man seems to cower before the vastness of nature, cringe before bigness, and feel enslaved by size. We need to understand that when man appreciates the One to Whom he belongs, he is no longer overwhelmed but instead is stirred by the mystery and wonder of life. Only man can contemplate nature and rejoice in its beauty, be awed before its majesty, shrink before its terrors.

In man nature becomes meaningful. A mountain does not recognize itself as a mountain and signal to the river that winds about its base. The Rockies are high, but they never break into song; the sea stirs the hearts of the sensitive, but it knows not the joy and grief of the lover nor the lonely loyalty of the martyr.

All meanings are read into nature by man. The universe cannot endow itself with value. A poem is but ink blotches upon paper until another man reads it and touches it into immortality; a political event, a scientific concept, has no meaning until man bestows it. Men enrich life with meaning that endures long after they are gone; but does the universe destroy the worker and preserve the works? Can it be that the song is greater than the singer and the thought more enduring than the thinker? Later in these pages we will find an answer.

So it is important for us to realize that only man of all creation is aware.

## THE THIRD PRINCIPLE: *Man Must Learn the Discipline of Duty to Know its Delight*

Babe Zaharias once told me that when she decided to become an expert golfer, she committed herself to hit 1,000 balls a day with one club. Ben Hogan once said he had to practice four hours a day to maintain his skill.

Some years ago I talked to a musician now known all over the world for his mastery:

"Do you practice regularly?"

"Yes, on the average of six hours a day."

"Do you love it?"

"Yes."

"Did you always love it?"

"No."

"Tell me about it."

"I was forced to practice until I could force myself to practice; I forced myself to do it until I loved to do it. Now I love to do it."

This is the experience of everyone who has achieved excellence in every walk of life. A young physician studied fifty hours a week during the first two years of medical school. Like the musician, he accepted the discipline of duty and then knew its delight. He finished with honors in his graduating class and was free to intern and do his residency in the hospital of his choice.

Excellence is not the mark of genius; it is the reward of blood, sweat and tears. It comes at a high price, but what a rare blessing it is! It means that one has taken this precious gift of life and given to it his best.

I do not want to convey the idea that the achieving of excellence is harsh toil alone. It is a most thrilling and important adventure. Never to attempt it is to miss the whole point of life; to court meaninglessness; to end up as a broken link in the divine plan of creation.

What one needs to realize is that while it is most meaningful and rewarding to fulfill one's destiny in the plan of creation, it is not easy. The end of the road is never in sight; one never arrives, at least in this dimension. The great achievements in all areas of life are costly. As one becomes a whole person, tangible achievements follow; excellence in every area of life becomes possible.

We need persons today who are governed from within themselves. Formal laws and statutes will not stand the stress imposed by men who have no dedicated loyalty to a goal which is worthy of their devotion and the devotion of all mankind. Laws and regulations can direct and complement but can never substitute for a personal sense of duty.

It is necessary to see that if a person is able to do what he should until he loves it, to accept the discipline of duty until he knows its delight, then in time he will be free to do what he wants to do.

So we are saying, in stating this third principle, that duty involves a fine discipline of the soul. There is a moral fiber that is developed by doing some things because they are right and because we ought to do them and for no other reason. He who acts only upon immediate, dominant impulses and never does anything out of superior motives, is destined not for the highest self-expression but for narrow self-limitation. The highest personal freedom issues from the sternest self-discipline. Only he who has enthroned law in the center of his soul will know true liberty. Then comes the delight of duty. Said the great musician, "I made myself do it until I loved to do it." Delight followed. Doing what we should, doing what demands the best in us, results in spontaneity and joy and a profound sense of mastery— a feeling that we are taking this gift of life and giving to it our all; that in a deep sense we are playing square with life.

The great purpose of law is to instill love of duty honored by choice. One man who accepted the discipline of duty until he knew its delight said, "Thy statute has become my own." What a thrilling insight! That which was once the discipline of duty on the outside is now melody at the very heart of life. Then one can say, "I am no longer a subject, I am a sovereign." This, then, is our third principle.

### THE FOURTH PRINCIPLE: *Out of Little Things Greatness is Made*

The real meanings of life are hidden in the heart of simplicity. The holy is ever an aspect of the homely and the mystery of the divine must be found in the apparent obviousness of the ordinary.

This principle is beautifully illustrated in the Christmas story. Government edicts, tax collectors, census-takers, a peasant family, a newborn child, shepherds watching their flocks—these are the elements in the simple story through which God revealed himself to man. It is the story of a man and a woman coming, at the end of a weary road, to a little town on a darkened hill, knocking in vain for shelter at a village inn, finding forlorn refuge in a stable. There in the dark of a winter's night, the outside world uncaring, the birth of a baby split the calendar and time became reckoned by His birth.

Is it not true that the great task for our lives is to conserve a saving simplicity? All about us people are losing their souls in the complexity of the world, where perspective is so easily lost. We need to go back to the simple and changeless principles of life, where truth is truth, love is love, virtue is not success but the high integrity of the soul, and life's rewards are not wealth and power but the soul's perception of the song of God's angels and the shining of His pilgrim star.

It is so strange that as our material satisfactions have increased and we have had more to eat and to wear, our anxieties have steadily increased, becoming sharper and greater. Fears have not decreased as material securities increased. We have come to feel that we can live by bread alone. But the very essence of virtue is one's ability to care for something above and beyond himself.

A long time ago this was brought home to me in a poem by Edith Gosling in which she said:

No star's caught in my hair? You're sure?
Look upward then and see if there's a halo hanging.
For surely something works this change,
In radiance.
Search my eyes—a glimmer, yes? Well, that's right,
Some universe within me, banded tight,
Burst its chains and swung its constellations through my being.[3]

Immoral life is governed by selfish, inward-directed desires and passions; moral life is goverened by an ideal directed both inward and outward—something calling and beckoning from the far horizons of life. It is this confusion of the secondary with the essential that so complicates life and drains it of its peace and stability. We adorn the frame and neglect the picture. We have an abundance of nonessentials, but a great shortage of the necessities for full living.

Out of the little things greatness is made; in simple things God reveals His glory; this is the principle that must guide us.

### THE FIFTH PRINCIPLE: *Every Problem is either Solvable or Transcendable*

This is more than a profound principle; it is a promise. Look at the life of Helen Keller who was born deaf and blind. Her problem was not solvable but she was able to transcend it. Jesus did not escape His cup. He prayed, "Let this cup pass from me; nevertheless, not as I will, but as thou wilt" (Matt. 26:39). It did not pass, but was transcended, turning defeat into victory. He drank the cup that today is a symbol to the world seeking to be born. He did not escape His cross, but He had the power and strength to make it the world's greatest throne.

Be sure of the truth of these words, "My grace is sufficient for you" (II Cor., 12:9). Every problem is either solvable or transcendable. You can either focus on your problem and become a part of it, or you can face your problem, move toward the solution, become a part of the solution and an inspiration to others.

As we go forward in this plan of research we see the profound truth that the person you can be you are now becoming, the one who is the fulfillment of your true destiny. There is a great momentum in life; at its very core there is longing. When a person is responsive to this longing, he is enroute, he responds to some tyrant dream that will not let him go.

This is true not only when the going is easy, when progress comes naturally, when the satisfactions are great and the disappointments few; it is true also when the going is difficult.

In fact, it is often the difficult that calls forth the very best in us.

Once a long time ago it struck me as particularly significant that in the heart of December is Christmas. For December is the chill of gray days—leaves once alive in green and gold, all withered and dry, blowing through the streets—gardens gone to their graves—the lone cry of birds in their search for summer climes—far off sunsets, cold. December is the year's end and the knowledge of hopes unrealized. Ships of souls that touched on our shores are gone, leaving desolate the harbor. Yet onward we go, perhaps more with dogged determination than with exuberant faith, wondering if life has meaning.

Winter in the world, star-like hopes faded from the sky, hatred trampling the flowers of grace and love; dark-drenched horizon; the muttering thunder of threatening storms; the threatened end of things that were beautiful and promising; tales of world domination by Godless dictators and nuclear warfare; an unknown tomorrow—December is here. But, again, in the heart of December is Christmas.

A poet, writing of Easter and all its heartening hopes, uttered a sentiment which inspires our faith and opens our heart again to Him who tells us, even though we cannot tell how the road will turn: "I will go with you to the end." The poet thinks of the tree, bleak and leafless, lifting bare beseeching arms to Heaven and he says:

> Undaunted by Decembers
> The sap is faithful yet;
> The growing earth remembers
> And only men forget.

Nature and history are never discouraged. Only men forget. Only human hearts, when caught in the lag, when unresponsive to visions of truth, sense no promise in December. Only man, when no longer inspired by the dream of what can be found in shipwreck and sorrow and defeat, sees the end of all things.

The blind plowman caught the spirit:

> Set my hands upon the plow,
> My feet upon the sod;
> Turn my face then toward the east
> And praise be to God—
> That God that made His sun to shine
> Alike on you and me;
> The God that takes away my eyes
> That now my soul may see.[4]

But how can we move from where we are, deceived by no false optimism, blinded by no easy and futile faith, expecting to go far in life's journey without paying our fare, counting on great results without meeting the requirements for them, assuming that a loving God will do it for us or that great things come by luck? How can we get beyond thinking that one can become a whole person merely by wishing to be and believing that the Holy Spirit will make us whole without our striving?

We will be seeing again and again that God's gift is infinite but it has no meaning without man's response. When we have His gift and man's response, then there are miracles. Then the impossible becomes possible. Then every problem is either solvable or transcendable.

## THE SIXTH PRINCIPLE: Love Must Be Linked with Restraint

If love is given without restraint, children can become impulse-governed and join the great army of sociopaths that plague our modern life. When love is freely given and when limits are firmly set, children become whole and can learn to set their own limits.

We can see this principle implied at work over and over as

we look around us. Many people want to do only what they want. But we know that a person can do what he wants only if he is also able to do what he does not want to do.

We see it in the attitude toward sin. Dr. O. Hobart Mowrer, Research Professor of Psychology at the University of Illinois, feels that the Freudian influence in America has undermined our whole moral structure by dealing only with guilt feelings but not with guilt. In the right view, there is judgment, but with compassion and understanding. Sin must be dealt with. Guilt must be recognized, else it will undermine the possessor's mental health, or lead him to projection onto others—to their injury.

We can see this principle in welfare work. If we help people to the extent of robbing them of the power of self-help, we hurt them. The same is true in world terms. The only way to be of help is to help people help themselves. Thus love and restraint mingle with each other.

## THE SEVENTH PRINCIPLE: *You and Every Other Person Must Begin Where You Are*

This is not always easy. Not to begin where you are means that you make a false start. The fact is that each person is always making a beginning. We have said that in all walks of life and in all states of being, persons are moving from where they are. They cannot stand still as long as they are alive at all.

The spirit of these pages is to grant each person the incentive to start from where he thinks he is, where he feels he is, where others have convinced him he is, or where in light of his past experience he assumes he is.

It is my feeling that with a plan of approach such as these pages outline, a plan of creative sharing in a personal growth group, or in other relations—if the starting point is false, the reader may come to see it. Moreover, he can find the freedom not only to see this, but to accept it, and start from where he truly is.

So we are saying that the important thing is to make a beginning and to keep trying until one finds the place he is and can move on from there.

In the next eight chapters we will describe how others found a true beginning. Much of what will be said includes the real stories of beginnings. We see the real beginning which is at conception; we see how to begin with creative fellowship. We see what happens when a "Radar Star" shines; when a thrust is provided; when symptoms seem real; when moral crises culminate; when time runs out and when awareness comes.

# CHAPTER 2.  WHEN LIFE BEGINS

What is the greatest moment of beginning for the person growing into wholeness of person and of body? It is the moment of conception.

Life is filled with mystery. Conception is part of the mystery. When you were conceived, you were a single cell, invisible to the naked eye. Yet in that cell was the essence of your body and of the reality that is you—the color of your eyes, the texture of your hair, the size and shape of your body and, to some degree, the nature of your feelings and patterns of response.

There is a deeper mystery. You are one of a potential four million persons. When your father and mother, being one in heart and mind, became one in body as a witness of their love, the gift of your father's body to your mother included about four million sperm. One penetrated the shell of the egg in your mother's womb and you came to be. Why was it you? Why was it I?

In that instant you came to be. This is the view I hold. I feel that in each conception, a new soul comes to be. There are those who believe in reincarnation and feel that while some souls are new creations, many return for another cycle, and that they enter the body at the moment of birth. While there are many reasons why this could be so, Jesus did not teach it and I never experienced it.

## THE RACIAL UNCONSCIOUS

Thus, conception to me is the beginning of a new soul and marks the real starting point. Of course, each of us without a doubt inherited something from the racial unconscious. It would seem there is a basis for belief in what has been called

13

"original sin." I accept this as long as it is not used as an excuse for not doing what love must do from the moment of conception.

Gerald Heard, one of my teachers in the life of prayer, feels that man fell not only once but a number of times. I have observed evidence for this. Why does man lose the freedom to grow? As William Sheldon, in *Psychology and the Promethean Will,* said, when a person arrives at the age when he can vote, he has stopped growing; he is like "a tree that is dead, except a few branches grow out of the trunk."[1] I have observed that many persons never recover this freedom to grow until just before they cross into the next dimension. Then, in an hour, they grow more than they have in a lifetime.

However, this loss is not a necessary one. When a person has a new spiritual experience, when he becomes a person, when he comes to know who he is, then he recovers the freedom to grow which he had as a child. Then he realizes that life is measured by the intensity of experience and not by the extension of time; it is measured not by the breaths taken but by those not taken— by the breath-taking experiences. He recovers the capacity to wonder, to dream, to ask, to seek, to know. He becomes teachable. He becomes like a child. Jesus never asked children to be like adults, but on a number of occasions he asked adults to become like children.[2]

Could this loss of the freedom to grow be one of the falls that occurred sometime in the distant past and therefore is part of the racial unconscious?

I have observed that just before a person expires, he often develops a profound perceptive capacity he never had in his life. Often he sees what he never saw; feels what he never felt; hears what he was deaf to. Was this not once man's capacity which he has lost?

One more factor has impressed me. Man seems to get confused between time and eternity. Across the centuries he has gone from one extreme to the other. At times he is too other-worldly, at other times so completely a victim of the present that he is without perspective.

## THE LIFE IN THE WOMB IS IMPORTANT

Over a period of many years, it has been my observation that the life in the womb influences the person beyond birth. Ashley Montagu, in his book *The Direction of Human Development*,[3] has carefully documented this.

If the parents love each other, if they feel affection, if they have a relationship in which their needs are met and their maximum growth insured, the baby is conceived in love and his life in the womb is peaceful. He is fully nurtured by the mother's blood, and her security and quiet confidence is communicated to the baby by her muscles and feelings. She knows joy and every cell of her body radiates this joy. The baby feels it. She is nurtured by love and the baby feels this love. Being loved, she can love her child before he is born.

The unborn baby is sensitive to outside disturbances. If an alarm clock goes off near the fetus, the unborn baby's heartbeat is accelerated.

If the mother is unloved and insecure; if the baby is unwanted; if she feels alone and in turmoil, the baby is bound to feel the influence, if no more than by neural irritation.

## IMPORTANCE OF PREPARATION FOR MARRIAGE

Never have young people been so interested in marriage and in love. Why this should be so is a phenomenon of great significance. Despite all the divorces and the many marriage failures they see, youth everywhere looks forward to marriage.

In fact, there has been an upsurge of teen-age marriages in the past decade. In 1958, 244,309 girls between the ages of fifteen and nineteen were married. This represents almost half of the women who were married in that year. Almost 1,900 of these wives were under fifteen years of age. In the same year, 30,175 boys between the ages of fifteen and nineteen were married. In 1958, 554,184 babies were born to girls in the fifteen to nineteen age group.

Why this upsurge in teen-age marriages? Some are unhappy in their homes. Many get pregnant and become married as one solution. Why do they get pregnant? Often they are lonely. They were never close spiritually to anyone so they get close physically and find themselves propelled by a momentum they can't control. Others are worried over the future and they want to taste of life as much as they can while they have a chance. Others feel helpless to do anything about their world and marry to create a little unit of the world of which they dream.

But teen-age marriages face real hurdles. They mean rushing out of the cradle to tending one; playing an adult role before the social and psychological adjustments are made through the stages of adolescence.

Preparation for marriage begins with conception. As the person grows from infancy, through the years of childhood and adolescence, into the early years of adulthood, he is getting ready for the relationship of marriage, a mosaic of the world dreamed of by millions of youth.

There are many hopeful signs today. Most colleges and universities have courses in marriage and the family; increasingly, clergymen are prepared to counsel young people from childhood to marriage; there are many helpful articles in magazines and an increasing number of good books on the subject.

Marriage can be joyous and fulfilling. Two people can become free for a great union in which children can be conceived in love, born in love, and grow up in love.

## SPECIFIC REQUIREMENTS FOR MARRIAGE

Knowledge is important. There is no relationship for which training is more needed than for marriage. Those who are to be truly wed and grow through union into wholeness as persons need training and the knowledge that implies.

But knowledge is not enough. Nor is insight enough. Two people must know who they are and understand themselves before they can understand each other. Then they can communicate with each other; they can work out their problems; they can take the hurdles; they can differ and still be close. But first they need to be free to love and be loved, both after the spirit and after the flesh. If they are close in feeling and in thought, then sexual closeness can have great meaning. Before the wedding and immediately after there may be a natural response of affection. There may be great readiness and eagerness to be close physically and this can be maintained if the other aspects of the relationship are well cared for. Now the relationship of affection and tenderness may change somewhat, but it needs to be kept alive. A couple needs to keep close spiritually so that in a deep sense they can be close physically. There needs to be fondness expressed in very personal and meaningful ways, not only in the intimate personal relations but in everyday relations—the thoughtful word, the little surprise, the remembrance, the expression of affection on parting and on being reunited. It is important, too, that a couple keeps alive the element of fun and romance. They go out, they do things together; their companionship is important. They share together, they communicate with one another, they are spiritually close. They love each other after the spirit, which gives meaning to love after the flesh.

It is important also that they keep vivid and vital their capacity to make love. It is possible for two people to maintain a relationship which keeps alive the capacity for desire. God gave them this amazing capacity for responding totally to each other. When they are thus drawn together, the union solves the problem of isolation. This is important for two reasons. If they have been apart physically, to come together gives each a feeling of special oneness and therefore cancels the feeling of separateness. If they have been psychologically separated, for one reason or another, the most healing thing in the world is for them to become one in body, for this seals the oneness of spirit and of mind.

In this connection it is important that they keep themselves physically attractive, which means keeping clean and neat, maintaining the right weight—giving thought to appearance as well as to the quality of thought and feeling. All of this lays the foundation for that total relationship in which lives are fulfilled and into which union a baby can come with all the hope in the world.

## THE BIRTH EXPERIENCE

The period of time from conception to birth provides an opportunity for the parents not only to grow closer, but to prepare for the coming of their first-born. In the spiritual laboratory where I worked for many years, we met with expectant parents to give them a chance to explore all aspects of their baby's development from that moment until it arrives. We found this to be a very worthwhile experience.

It is true that most hospitals have classes for the young mother after the baby is born. In some situations the father is included. This chance to meet with other couples and to grow in understanding and insight before the coming of the baby is very helpful.

All couples are not ready for the experience of parenthood. It is best for them to choose the time when the new life will start. Many couples, unless they marry late in life, prefer to control conception by whatever method is in line with their belief or which their physician recommends. There is wisdom in this. They then have a chance to learn to live together. Up to the wedding day persons often relate on an emotional level; they are expectant and therefore elated. After they pass this peak and settle down to everyday life, they begin to live on the level of their habit system.

Even though they may have had a reasonable dating and engagement period, even though they were taken through a sound study period before the wedding, they never know each other so well as when they begin to live together, when they see each other every morning before breakfast. Then they react as they are. Disillusionment can easily come when the young husband sees the contrast between his wife's ways and his mother's. It can threaten him, lead him to feel, "Home was never like this." Likewise with the wife. Her father might have been one to wake up early, sing in the shower, go around pounding his chest and saying, "What a day!" Her husband may wake up slowly, give her the silent treatment, and after a month of marriage go off to work without a kiss or a word. Can't you hear her say, "Home was never like this"?

The best marriage counseling I ever did was after the wedding, after the couple had had laboratory experience. If the two people have enough time before the wedding; if they come out of healthy family relations; if they have a chance for thorough premarital study, the first year of marriage can be more satisfactory. They have understanding and freedom to deal with the areas where they need to grow in order to work toward maximum fulfillment. They find it easier to accept each other as they are, see each other as they can be, and go on from there.

In the early months of a marriage, there may be stress over finding sexual fulfillment. Most couples find that if they accept what meaning it has for them and grow from there, that meaning increases across the years. Family influences, dependencies on parents which they can transfer to each other, the need to be a little girl or boy rather than a husband or wife, a neurotic need to save or a compulsive need to spend, temperamental factors and mood swings, values and ways of doing things, basic appreciations and tastes, capacities to listen and to respond—all are important in their relationship.

So if a couple has time to grow into a relationship before conceiving a child, it is good; for when pregnancy occurs, it sometimes creates new areas of stress. If the husband needs his wife to mother him or if she has a need to do so, the coming baby can threaten him. A competitor is on the way. If a wife is in a little girl role, the prospect of motherhood can be both pleasurable and anxiety-producing. She may have concern about the experience of giving birth. All of these problems need understanding and interpretation.

A couple also needs to plan for the child together, to learn of its care, to acquire insight which will take them through the early weeks of their life with the little one. They can come to see that they need something to love together in order to grow in love for each other.

The nearer the great moment comes, the closer they should be. As the hour approaches, they go to the hospital together. Some hospitals allow the husband to be with his wife through the birth experience. There is a growing feeling that after the baby is born, it should be in the same room with the mother. The birth experience is a shock to the new life; it was secure for nine months; now it is out of the womb and alone; it needs to be close to the mother, in her arms a good deal at first. With this relationship, her body fulfills its functions better.

In time, mother and child come home and the three now begin their life together. What an amazing experience it can be!

## A FINAL WORD

If for one generation family relationships could be such as to meet basic need and foster continuing growth, most mental illness and much physical illness could be eliminated. For healthy minds and healthy bodies are the only ramparts to peace the world knows.

Of what worth is anything else if we keep not a faithful watch over the cradle of a child in the first days of its existence? Apart from this, science and learning, government and religion are nothing. With this, God would come again in every child and make each home a Bethlehem.

A baby at birth is fresh from the creative hands of God. It is not disorganized; it is highly organized, all ready for love and to love.

Jesus loved all men and set for them spiritual goals and pictured for them methods of love. It is breathtaking to remember that once there was another Jewish boy born into a home. This boy loved the mass of men, too, but he chose for them economic

goals and ordered methods of violence. His name was Karl Marx.
Today the followers of these two leaders are pitted against each
other.

Two boys were born in Austria. One decided he would live
his life for beauty, and he put songs into the hearts of millions.
The other chose power and he struck panic into the hearts of
millions. One was Beethoven; the other was Hitler. Think of
the promise of a baby. Think of the peril of a baby. The entire
universe is organized and planned to help each baby grow up
with the spirit that can lead him to maximum fulfillment. And
if our homes and our churches and our communities and our
schools do their duty, each child's true heritage may be realized.
He can be not only the hope of the world but he can meet the
requirements for a world that must be free.

# CHAPTER 3. WHEN FELLOWSHIP IS CREATIVE

Man is now at a point in his development from which he can grow only in fellowship. There is no salvation alone. Why do we have schools, colleges and universities, churches and synagogues, numberless interest groups? Growth is initiated and continues in fellowship. Because of fellowship a person can carry on alone.

I have never seen any person go very far alone, either in his educational enterprise or in his own spiritual growth. The great progress I've seen has been among people who found themselves in a creative relationship with one person or with a group. They began to find understanding in such a relationship; they found a starting point; they were motivated to begin dealing with their problems and continued as a result of the inspiration of the group. The group called to the best in them and they made their best contribution in response.

There is a growing recognition that therapy is most successful in fellowship. A recent book, *The Couch and the Circle*,[1] presents a story of group psychotherapy in which troubled people help and heal themselves and each other. On the flap there appeared these words: *"By the crowd they have been broken; by the crowd shall they be healed."* I question the universal truth of this. For some persons it is true, for others not.

Even in counseling the important thing is the relationship between the counselor and the person seeking freedom. I have seen healing take place in relations where accepted methods of counseling were in process; I have seen it take place where the counselor was directive, where he broke all the rules of counseling, where he preached, and went all-out to provide outer motivation. I have even seen people improve after they made a date for a conference. Recently I heard William B. Oglesby, Jr., Professor of Pastoral Counseling at Union Theological Seminary, Richmond, Virginia, say, "After a student says, 'I need to to see you,' I say, 'I want to see you, but my schedule is full until Tuesday of next week at 4:00.' Occasionally, when the time comes, the student arrives and says, 'I guess I don't need to see you; I got it worked out on my own.'" Why? Professor Oglesby cared. For a moment the student knew that someone cared; for a moment he wasn't alone; for a bit he was in the circle of loving concern. It was enough. Then he could go it alone.

The Bible says, "Bear one another's burdens" (Gal. 6:2). It also says, "Each man will have to bear his own load" (Gal. 6:5). We are made for fellowship. Jesus knew this and therefore put much emphasis on it. "This is my commandment, that you love one another as I have loved you" (John 15:12). "You are my friends if you do what I command you" (John 15:14).

## THERE ARE TWO KINDS OF FELLOWSHIP

There is a force that makes for fellowship. If the cells of the body are healthy, they make for fellowship. In a real sense your body is a brotherhood of cells. Something draws a baby to its parents and parents to the baby, a girl to her crowd, a boy to his gang and a boy to a girl. Some powerful force has been drawing people together until the world has become a neighborhood.

In *The Cocktail Party,* T. S. Eliot suggests that the reason the cocktail glass has become so important is that the communion cup has lost its meaning. I have been to cocktail parties where people got so close physically and so free emotionally that basic relationships between husbands and wives were threatened. I have, of course, been to some that were on a high level, where the closeness was not physical or superficial. But the communion cup represents a special relationship in which persons become close in fellowship and yet are most fully themselves. They find the mastery of Him who is Lord.

Thus the nature of fellowship is important. When persons become close, when they not only rub shoulders but hearts, when they are loved and understood, when they feel tenderness, then healing comes; then they can become whole.

Howard Thurman says, "One of the dismal heritages from the past is the widespread disintegration of tenderness which makes us falter, hesitate and become immobile in our efforts to understand each other and to deal with each other sympathetically. It is true that there is a kind of understanding abroad, but it is an understanding that invades, threatens, makes afraid or embarrasses. We have made an idol of togetherness which takes the form of a muted mass hysteria. Togetherness in a sense is a watchword of our times. It seems that more and more it is a substitute for God. In the great collective huddle we are lonely, desolate, frightened."[2]

Anyone who is sensitive to other persons realizes that there is an emotional aloneness, a homesickness of soul, that is widespread. It springs from many sources. It is due in part to the movement of people from one place to another. In part, it is the result of a world in terrible travail, a world in which millions can merely exist. Millions of children are orphaned, fathers and mothers are separated, husbands work away from home. In many families both husband and wife work. Moreover, we have put such a premium on becoming a part of the group that this becomes the prime goal and the individual is lost in the herd. He, as we said in the Introduction, loses his own identity. He has no sense of being.

Perhaps a more fundamental cause of this aloneness is the vastness of the universe. There's a sense of homelessness engendered by the very bigness of things. As we said in Chapter 1, many people cower before the vastness of nature.

This reminds us of the need for the right kind of fellowship. When people become close to each other, when they have a relationship that calls to the best in each, and each calls to the best in the group, then there is a sense of being. Then it is possible for the person to come to know the One to Whom he belongs. Then is the individual at home in his universe. No longer is he a cosmic orphan, but a part of the Divine Presence.

It is difficult for him to come to this sense of God if he is far from people. That is why Jesus again and again made clear that we can't be in a wrong relationship with people and close to God. You remember He even said, "So if you are offering your gift at the altar, and there remember that your brother has something against you, leave your gift there before the altar and go; first be reconciled to your brother, and then come and offer your gift" (Matt. 5:23).

Nothing is so vital as to be a part of a creative fellowship where you can be your real self and still feel accepted and loved. Then it's possible for you to respond to the nameless longings that ever lure you onward.

After all, the deepest satisfactions in life beget the deepest longings. The tenderest human love with its comradeship is the haven in which the ships of desire might rest, but it is also a harbor from which they set sail for the calling deeps. A philosopher once walked by the seaside with a young woman and listened to her talk of love and its beauty. Suddenly she stooped to pick up a pebble glinting white and green and gold, and she showed it to him. As they walked on, she told of her faith in love and its power to fulfill one completely. But the philosopher said, "Show me the pebble again, the one your hand holds so tightly." She reached out her hand and revealed it, not shining and beautiful but dull and dry. "There," he said, "you see, you must not pick up pretty pebbles if you do not want them to lose their luster; you must leave them where the waters of the ocean can roll over them." Going back, the young woman replaced her pebble upon the beach. Her face was not happy until she had seen the waves break over it, bathe it, and then recede. These human loves of ours are sources of deep satisfaction; they give us great joy and show their richest colors when they are overswept by the mysterious tide of an infinite sea.

The longing of love that comes so sharply in the gray days of bereavement is always within us. The truest love is the merging of the infinite longing of two human souls. It is not always the cure of the soul's loneliness. It is comradeship in loneliness.

Suffering and longing and agony are at the core of all human experience; the spirit of man confesses itself a stranger upon the earth. Indeed, when man no longer is disquieted, he no longer feels within himself the restlessness of one athirst; he has ceased to be human and his soul has become a desert. It is the lost soul that feels no pang of great desire, nor the hurt of noble discontent. In Part II we will elaborate this more in detail for it is one of the unfailing resources of our very nature. It is basic to our fullest becoming.

## SOME GROUP EXPERIENCES

Let us now look at some group experiences to see how important they are. Some, I'm sure, are akin to those that you have had. When a group becomes alerted, when individuals become free to respond to their deep feelings, when they become free to say what they think, to get beyond the veneer and the role they have been playing in response to group expectations, then something happens. There is a breakthrough; they become alert and they find a point of real beginning.

1. *An Experience with a College Group.* Recently I met with a group of young people who were back home from college. They all had known each other well before they went away to school. A few of them attended college in their home town. I had never met them before. They were called together by a few eager adults.

We met in a home. There were perhaps forty of them present. After we ate and shared casually with each other, they were asked to sit on the floor. I was given a place to sit and then I was introduced.

I made a brief opening statement about the human condition, the attitudes of young people whom I had known and what could happen when a group really became awakened. The immediate response came from the more negative ones, the agnostics and the atheists. A few felt that the communists had the real answer.

For an hour and a half they overwhelmed me. There were some clever people there. They were brilliant. They were quick on the uptake. At the end of the hour and a half my armor was dented. It was perfectly plain that nothing I could say would ever influence them. As I watched their faces, I could see that a number—perhaps ten or fifteen per cent of the group—were not in sympathy with this point of view. They looked kindly. They were sympathetic, but they were silent. One or two spoke up, but what they said was not heard. The eloquent ones were anti-Christianity, anti-religion, anti-church and everything the church stood for. They were actually against America, against the free world.

Sensing the situation, I did not try to argue with them. I did not endeavor to convince them. I simply began giving them back their feelings and their thoughts. When a girl said, "Anybody who believes in God is senile," I said, "You feel for one to believe in God means that he is either very immature or is coming to the end of his life and has therefore lost his hold on himself."

When we concluded, the group just broke up. They were frankly distraught, anxious, and nervous. Some of them were embarrassed and even some of the most eloquent were unhappy about what had taken place. More than likely the thing that frustrated them most was that I didn't fight back or get defensive, and that I kept smiling and giving them back their views.

After they were gone, a few of those who were not in sympathy with the negations apologized. The adults who had gathered the group were embarrassed. I listened to them a while and then said, "Most of those young people didn't mean what they said. They were simply taking on a role that they came to accept in their colleges."

I went on to say, "Why don't we get them together, a small group at a time, say six or eight, for luncheon. Pick them carefully so that you get congenial groups, inviting those who have been close in the past."

This we began to do. Strangely enough, when we got them together in small groups, they were not agnostic; they were not negative. The adult leaders who had met with me in the beginning were amazed. Now these young people were open and searching; now their true selves came to be shown. At the end of the summer we planned a week-end retreat. They came together, no longer negative and agnostic, but searching, loving, open, responsive.

They met in small groups. They came back and reported, and I shared with them. The interchange between us and with some of the adult leaders was a thrilling and wonderful experience.

At the summer's end they stood together in a circle and sang a piece I love very much, "Peace I Ask of Thee, O Father," and then we went around the circle and each one offered a prayer. I closed the prayer, and before they broke the circle a number of them said, "We have become free to be ourselves with each other; now tell us how can we go back and create the same relationship in our colleges this fall."

We spent as much time as we could helping them to see what they could do. They had come to know that when the right relationship is developed, individuals become free to be the persons they really are, and then fellowship becomes a creative experience.

2. *A Group of Men.* I was invited to meet with a group of eighty men some time ago. We met at a beautiful place, arriving in time for dinner on Saturday evening. Later we met in a parlor, sitting around in soft chairs. Their minister introduced me and said I would now talk to them. Instead, I said to them, "Before I talk I would like to listen to you. If I talk now it will be from where I am, but if you begin, then later I can talk from where you are. I would like you to start here at the right and go around the group, each one saying where he is in his own growth, what problems he is facing, what his frustrations are, what his difficulties are, where he might begin to become the person he would really like to be."

In order not to put pressure on them, I said, "Now you're

free to pass if you wish." The first one did pass. The second one spoke timidly and with some hesitation, but gradually each man became more and more free, feeling the support of his friends. The freer they became, the more they talked from the depths of their hearts. Repeatedly the minister suggested a coffee break, but they refused. We began about 8:30 and continued until midnight. Each time he asked them to stop for coffee they said, "No, this is the first time we've had a chance to talk. If we stop for a coffee break we'll never get back to it." They continued until each man had said what was in his mind and heart.

The remarkable thing is that each man became free to say what he really thought. Again and again one man would say to another, "Why, Jim, I never knew you felt like that." "Bill, I never dreamed that this is the way you felt." You see, they had always responded on the basis of what they thought was expected. They were a part of this collective huddle. They were lost in the group stereotypes. They were responding to the herd. They were being the persons others wanted them to be.

Now they became free. Each man was able to be himself in a group and still feel accepted and understood.

At the close, we stood in a circle and many of them prayed. Later some said that they had never before prayed in public. Man after man turned to his minister and said, "I've loved you, but so much of the time I haven't understood what you've been talking about." What the minister was really doing was giving them a set of words. He was trying to give them God in words and not in experience. Now these men found a relationship in which they became sensitive, not only to each other but to God.

They formed a committee to organize their concerns into areas. The next morning they formed small groups to meet around these areas and again their leaders had trouble persuading them to adjourn. For the first time they were talking; they were being listened to with understanding; each man was beginning to know how he felt and why. They were talking and they were being listened to in such a way that, in a deep sense, they understood what they were saying and what they were feeling.

They were discovering that one has to be listened to carefully. Then, in time, one can listen to others with understanding and appreciation. Finally they returned to the entire group and began to report. I led them as they shared with each other, as they pooled their wisdom. And as they responded to each other, I summarized and gave my own view. But my view now was given in terms of where they were rather than where I was.

When they came to the conclusion of their meeting they said, "We have just begun." They agreed to meet once a week with their wives, carrying on the research program they laid out, and to make a record for the benefit of others. For a year and a half they have continued. I have had letters from them and their wives relating the positive results.

3. *A Group of Women.* Many years ago I invited a group of women to meet and asked if they would like to carry out a program of spiritual research so that they could come to know who they were, understand who they were, and then meet the requirements for creative and vital human relations.

I invited them because I found that only on this basis could I get the people who should come. Jesus did not announce in the Galilee newspaper that all who were interested in the Kingdom of God should come to a fish fry. He invited them one at a time. I did the same with this group of women. At the same time I reported in our publication the fact that if anyone was interested in becoming a part of a group, she was to let me know.

This group of women began to meet and have continued to over the years, growing in insight and in understanding. Today they are outstanding women, not only in terms of this particular group, but in the city where they live. It is remarkable what happened to them as they shared with each other. They became women with a true sense of selfhood.

4. *A Group of Couples.* In the same church, more than twenty years ago, I invited ten couples to meet with my wife and me and

another couple who were part of the staff. We met in the Y.W.C.A. for a simple meal. After we had our meal and talked for a while, I said something like this: "Something happens when you come to the hour of worship and listen to me preach. But I'm positive that greater things can happen when we meet in a small group where you can talk, listen to each other, and share with each other. Moreover, we live in a time when we rub elbows with many but do not get really close. It occurred to me that you might want to meet and continue to meet until you become close, until you find a way of life that has real meaning. There is no limit to the extent of the research you can carry on. It is up to you. I will work with you. I will serve as a resource leader as much as I can."

They were startled. When it became clear what I was actually saying to them, they began to respond. They began to admit that they were hungry for just this thing. They wanted to become a part of a real research group. They wanted to find a faith they could live by; they wanted to find a way of life that was real. They wanted to be persons; they wanted their families to find the best possible relationships; they wanted to be creative citizens in the world.

The fact is that this group is still together, still meeting. It has been meeting nearly twenty years. Couples have moved out of the city and new couples have been added. But some of the original members are still a part of the group. They've never become a clique; they've never become ingrown. They *have* grown in wholeness of person and body, and this is reflected in their families, in their vocational life, in their churchmanship, in their citizenship, in their vision, in their capacity to be themselves in every relationship of life.

5. *A Group of Twelve Men.* Twenty years ago I invited twelve men to come to our home and presented to them a proposition similar to that which I made to the group of couples I just described. They responded. That group is still meeting. More than a hundred men have come and gone and a number have stayed. They have become a creative and redemptive and expan-

sive group. They have provided men of insight for all kinds of leadership within the spiritual laboratory of which they were a part and their leadership is now spread out across the nation.

## WHEN BONDS ARE BROKEN

In subsequent chapters we will describe points of beginning of people in various stages of growth, but in order to give emphasis to the power of the creative group, let me give here three stories of the creative power of a group for the healing of a person.

Dr. O. Hobart Mowrer reported in a group recently the story of a woman who had been in a state of obsessive anxiety for a long time, and of how she became a part of a group of people who were also troubled, distraught and broken.

This woman became free in the group to unburden her soul, to confess the life she had lived, which had been against the universe and in violation of her true nature. At first she hesitated, but gradually she opened her heart and bared her soul. As she did, she was not rejected by the group; she was accepted, she was loved, she was upheld.

This did not mean that they condoned her wrongdoing. They said that she had done wrong, but that she was wise to confess it, and that they would help her insofar as they could to undo the wrong she had done. They made judgments with compassion and understanding.

Dr. Mowrer went on to report that she went further and confessed to her husband. This she had previously been afraid to do, thinking he would reject her completely. Finding courage in being accepted by the group, she went a step further and cleared the record with her husband. To her amazement, he now came to her with new warmth, new understanding, new feeling.

Being free from guilt, she was able to remove the wall that separated her from him and from other people. She is now in fellowship. She can live with herself; she can look at herself and feel secure. She came to know wholeness and healing.

This woman's experience brings to my mind that of a man who passed me one morning after a service in our church. He was deeply moved and could not talk. I asked him to wait for a bit, which he did. I gave him an appointment to see me. When he came he could not talk, so we arranged another meeting. He came a second time and again could not talk, so I sat with him and was quiet with him and loved him. Finally I asked if he would be interested in joining a group of men who were meeting together. He nodded that he would.

The group had great freedom. They were searching together. They were moving from where they were to where they could go. Each had made a good beginning, and they were going forward in fellowship. That night one man confessed to some unfinished business in his life, and when he concluded the group responded, accepted him and assured him of forgiveness. It was an evening of great warmth. Their closeness permitted a sense of God in their midst.

They were standing for their closing ritual, when this man finally found his courage. He was able to talk. He said, "Could you wait a little? I need to talk."

Then he unburdened his soul: once he had had death fantasies about a brother who later had committed suicide. This had been fifteen years ago. Part of him had been glad his brother was gone and part of him felt guilty. He had bottled up these feelings and the result was an ulcer. Over a fifteen-year period he had paid one physician $3,000 to treat his ulcer, but unfortunately the physician had not treated the real cause.

As he told the whole story he broke into a cold sweat. The men loved him. They did not rush up and touch him, but they loved him and accepted him; he was a man in their presence. When he finished his story, they said, "What you wished for was wrong, but you can be forgiven." One of them read from the sixth chapter of Matthew, and when he had finished, another said, "Now you have one job left: you must forgive yourself. If you forgive yourself, then you can be forgiven and restored to union." I supplemented this. He began to relax; he looked like a new person.

Then someone said, "Perhaps you ought to choose a new doctor." This he did. The new doctor hospitalized him and made a careful medical study. He put him on a diet. He had never before followed his diet, but now he did. He no longer needed to punish himself; go to Calvary for himself. Now he could recognize the fact that someone had done it for him, that God was ready to forgive him the moment he could face it and deal with it and finally forgive himself.

My third story is the summary of the experience of a couple in a group. This couple had been brought by another which had been in the group for some time. The man was distraught with fear and the wife was filled with resentment. Vocationally her husband was a failure.

They were restrained at first, but as they began to share in the group, feeling the freedom and the closeness and the warmth, the husband finally said, "I've gone to church all my life, but religion isn't real to me. I've never really understood what the minister was saying. I've sung in choirs and gone to church only because I love music." The wife then spoke up and said, "Well, I'm too resentful to go to church. Things are going from bad to worse for us. We've tried to live according to the rules, but things are getting worse. To be very frank with you, I came tonight only to be polite. I decided I would never be caught in a church again, but I must say there is something about this group that I have never felt before."

Neither said anything more. However, the next day the wife came to see me and unburdened her soul. Later I arranged to see her husband and we began to work through their financial plight. They were in such a serious situation that they did not have enough for their Thanksgiving dinner. The church arranged to give them some help.

They continued to grow in the group, becoming free, alive

and radiant. In due time one of the members of the group was able to open a new vocational opportunity for the husband. He did more than this—he spent time with him and helped him overcome his anxiety. He was fidgety and tense. He started things but didn't follow through. Gradually the husband's vocational life improved, his vocational role became more satisfying, and the financial burden became lighter.

Today both the couple and their children reflect the improved relationships that have been developing within their family life. The husband, while not wealthy, has satisfying work. He is able to make enough money to meet their needs. The wife is taking a creative and joyful role in many of the volunteer agencies of the community. Her activities are not a way of escape from herself but a way of giving witness to her life and her wholeness.

If you were to ask, they would say that their new life started as a part of a live group. From there, they were able to "go it alone."

# CHAPTER 4. WHEN A "RADAR STAR" SHINES

Persons make a real beginning in the right relationship with others and they grow from there. Many persons got their start through the influence of a person in whose presence they became alive, alerted and jarred into taking stock, and thus were helped to move from where they were.

Gerald Heard once said that every person needs a teacher—but before he is ready for a teacher, he needs to be challenged by one who is a "radar star." This term comes from Edwin Hubble, the great astronomer, who stated that of all his explorations of the heavens and the immense reality of an expanding universe, the most startling discovery was that of the "radar star." Some of these stars have no mass at all and yet reflect compelling radiation power.

We have all had experiences with people who are "radar stars." They have changed the course of our lives. In their presence we've come alive. Something about them made us aware of the weak spots in our lives and gave us the impetus to do something about them.

These are the people who radiate ceaselessly though we may not always notice it. Jacob, when he awoke from his dream, said, "Surely the Lord is in this place; and I did not know it" (Gen. 28:16). Such people come to know, not only who they themselves are, but more importantly the person they can love —and their love is not withheld. From there, love moves on like a chain reaction to others.

What a blessing it is to us and to the future of the race that there are men and women of such insight—not lonely seers, nor persons cut off from life and out of touch with humanity, but people who are a part of the human stream. Their touch, their intuitive understanding, their invisible communion with the soul is so deep and so sure that, while it may not always be noticed, there are those who become aware of it and thereafter can never be the same. They begin to grow from there. But for these people, these "radar stars," the succession of men of good will would be broken. They are individuals of such integrity, such sincerity, that the intention and the act, the will and the performance are one. They are in the process of being reborn, and because of their willingness to live for others, we are reborn too. They are here in order to give us a transfusion of their courage, their honor, their insight and their dedication. We are infused with the spirit and are brought along in the same stream of eternal life. We just can't be the same. We can't stand still. They jar us and we start there.

Jesus came among the mass of humanity and called men to a regal independence. He declared that all Heaven is concerned with the destiny of a human soul. When this truth became really felt, man stood erect as never before and became aware of the gift of his being and the infinite potential of his becoming.

The spirit grew from Jesus through a group of His disciples and followers. It moved from person to person, from group to group, until—after three hundred years—the tyranny of the Roman Empire was overcome.

Today most of what we deeply prize in our republic came from that lonely, unique Galilean who was and is the world's greatest "radar star." The love that was so eloquent in Jesus, that grew from Him through person to person to overcome the tyranny of Rome, can renew itself in us and grow until a mighty momentum turns the tide from war to peace and gives hope to the suffering masses of the world.

It has always been true that on the rim of the wide world there rises the spires of a civilization whose bulwarks are righteousness and truth. The greatest glory of the earth are those souls who, in all generations, follow the gleam—defeated, scorned, trampled, crushed under the chariot wheels of the world. But they rise and go forward—praying, hoping, believing, singing a song that echoes across the world: "This one thing we do, we press on; we count not ourselves to be apprehended. God has concealed a truth; we must find it; the lure of it is the passion of our souls."

And you can see them climbing toward the dawn; Savonarola, St. Francis of Assisi, John Hampden, Wilberforce, Elizabeth Fry, John Newman, Abraham Lincoln. And before them all, one about whom there lingers the shadow of the cross.

These are the "radar stars." Some of them were brilliant. They shine across the pages of history. Others, perhaps not as brilliant, yet provide illumination to individuals whose lives they touch. Individuals who recognize such "radar stars" can no longer be the same; they make a beginning; they start where they are and move in the direction that they must go if they are to be true to their destiny.

## BEING PERSONAL

As I look back over my life I see here and there these "radar stars." I came in touch with them; I walked into their light; things became clear; I could no longer be the same.

One was Silas Orris, a teacher in a little country school in Pennsylvania. One night he asked me to remain after the others had gone. He said, "You should go to high school." I made up my mind to follow his advice, and it changed the whole course of my life.

One day while I was teaching in a high school in Mechanicsburg, Pennsylvania, a man said to me, "You should give your life to church leadership of young people." I'd always had a deep feeling that God wanted me in the ministry but I resisted it.

This man was E. H. Bonsall, then a director of young people's work for the Pennsylvania Sabbath Schools' Association. When he said this, it jarred me, but it opened a door. I could no longer stand where I stood. In due time, the way was opened for me to become youth leader for the then United Brethren

Church. From there I went to the International Council of Religious Education where I served for eight years, and during this time got my Master's and Ph.D. degrees at the University of Chicago. God used E. H. Bonsall to help me be discontent with what I was. I had to start there, and it proved to be a great beginning.

After I came to the church where I served many years, I was asked to go to Newcastle, Pennsylvania, to be on the program of the annual convention of the Pennsylvania Council of Churches. I had read a number of books by F. W. H. Meyers of London, who was also on the program. I went to hear him, for I wanted to see the man whose words had so much meaning for me. When first I saw him, I was disappointed, for his appearance was not impressive. In fact, I thought someone had come to take his place. When I was later told that it was he, I began to listen, even though at first I wasn't interested. But the longer I listened, the more something happened to me. I no longer saw him, but actually felt I saw the Lord. It was a moving experience, and frankly I've never been the same since.

When he had finished and the session was concluded, I went to him and asked him to have lunch with me. At the luncheon I said, "How did you get this way? Something happened to me while you were speaking that never happened before. I lost sight of you and saw the Lord." His remark will always be vivid to me, for he said, "I prayed three hours this morning for that to happen to someone."

I kept asking him, "How did you get this way? What happened to you? How is it that you seem to be so alive with the spirit of Jesus Christ?" He finally said this, "When I served a church in London many years ago, a very attractive minister came to a church nearby. He became a sensation. Many of the people who had been coming to hear me left and went to hear him. This created anxiety in me and led ultimately to resentment. It was a major spiritual problem for me. The more I resented him, the more ineffective I became.

"Finally I went off to be alone and I wrestled with the Lord from Monday to Friday. Finally He gave me a victory and the victory was this: I could honestly say, 'Dear Lord, send G. Campbell Morgan so many people to hear him that those who can't get in will come to hear me.' I went back to my church and in due time it filled up. I learned one lesson from the experience—that I must be alive with the Lord; I must know prayer power if I was to be free to bear witness to His spirit."

I never forgot that. F. W. H. Meyers was a "radar star." He forced me to make a new beginning, and at that moment I committed my life to a life of prayer.

I had heard of Gerald Heard, and once, during a speaking engagement in Los Angeles, had an opportunity to meet him. A friend of his took me sixty miles from Los Angeles to a place called Trabuco, where we were to meet this great master of the spirit at one o'clock. We were at the gate in plenty of time. I shall never forget seeing him come down the path from a high hill. As I stood there, I deeply sensed that I met him before he arrived. He approached the gate and I noticed that his eyes were like none I have ever seen—they were alive and vital; I felt that they saw through me, but I did not mind. When he came to the gate, we shook hands and I felt that we met totally. Just as God is totally present, so was Gerald Heard.

He came outside of the gate and we sat in a car. I had no conversation in mind, so I said, "Let us be still." We were; it was the most eloquent silence I ever heard in my life. In time I said, "Please talk to me," and the fact is that he began to talk to the point of my very need.

I was with him an hour and I've never been the same since. It was another point of beginning and it was not a false start. I made new commitments to do research in the life of the spirit, to learn prayer power, to find its meaning and lead others into the prayer path and into prayer research.

One day I got a letter from a man by the name of Paul Brunton saying that he was going to be in Dayton, Ohio, and was led to ask me to meet him. I am ashamed to admit that I was arrogant. I answered that if he was led to see me, he should come to Columbus, which he did. When we met he said that he was led to offer to be my teacher in the life of the spirit. I accepted his offer, for after being with him, I felt that here was one of the most highly developed spiritual persons I'd ever met. He, too, was indeed a brilliant "radar star."

For eight years when he came to Columbus once or twice a year, we spent time together. I read every book he wrote. He provided the relationship which made possible new beginnings for me. In fact, I made beginning after beginning for, in the deepest sense, each day is a point of new beginning. We never arrive; we are ever enroute. The important thing is to make a beginning, and one of the ways we do this is through knowing a person who is a "radar star." His light is so clear and so warm and so brilliant that we see where we are; we get a vision of where we can go and we have a chance to begin.

## THINK OVER YOUR LIFE

Think back over your own life—whether you've lived a few years or many—and point to those who touched your life at a given moment. If something happened to you, if you were never the same afterward, this is reason to hope for more.

If you're stuck, if you're in a state of lethargy or hopelessness, search out someone in whom you can have faith—someone who could be your teacher, in whose presence you could be yourself with confidence and with faith. If he is the right person and if you are ready, then you will make a beginning and you will keep going. The longer you keep going, the more confidence you will have of passing the point of no return.

Moreover, as you make a beginning and keep going, there is every chance that you yourself will become a "radar star." You will be the one in whose fellowship others can find a point of beginning, the faith and the inspiration to start and to keep going. Thus a chain reaction will be started that can change the whole world.

# CHAPTER 5. WHEN A THRUST IS PROVIDED

For many people, a point of beginning is initiated by what we might call a "thrust." An experience stirs the awakening and becoming the motivating power to get the person to move from where he is and begin to grow into wholeness. But before we elaborate this, we need to understand the nature of the bonds which block growth.

## MANY ARE FREE TO GROW

Many are free to grow, many are out of prison, many know who they are. Some have grown naturally from the moment of conception. Perhaps they started with the advantage of inherited stability and inborn gifts that came to crown their life. Maybe also they had a security-producing life in the womb. They may have been born out of love and into love. These are the really fortunate persons, and this is the kind of start we hope can be our gift to future generations of children.

Throughout babyhood and the power-struggle years from the time they could walk, these fortunate few had parents who were neither perfectionists and coercive nor permissive, but provided the right balance of tenderness and gentleness and restraint. They moved up through childhood, learning to share with children not so blessed, some of whom may already have been suffering under actual tyranny. Some had enough health in their situation to become superior persons, the key leaders in their group, the "shapers," those who mold behavior, those who are at once the "chosen ones." They grew into puberty with understanding and with healthy feelings. They moved through the seasons of adolescence with increasing insight and with growing appreciation and skills: learning how to be a part of a group but still retaining personal integrity; being able to love but free to set limits in heterosexual relations because of their spiritual closeness with those in the home; learning to travel the roads of destiny which we will describe in Part III; drawing upon the unfailing resources which we will evaluate in Part II.

Others began in a poor relationship but found a starting place later and became emancipated and grew into wholeness.

There are many of these persons, some more free and whole than others. But for them life would cave in all about us; without them everything we cherish would indeed be in jeopardy. These are the most hopeful among us; these are the ones who respond most quickly to opportunities for even greater spiritual growth. The tragedy is that our world sets up many barriers to this continued growth. Many starts are made but the process is so often held up.

In scientific research we know how to start with a problem, carry it through to a solution and then make the solution into a significant gift to our common life—or perhaps into a threat to the life of man on the earth. But in the realm of human relations, we move in *spurts*, we make starts but we have not learned how to carry through steadily. Persons may grow only so far before they face conflict with group standards and forms of behavior. And so they often settle down and become shaped by the stereotypes, or they join the "shapers," contributing thus to the cult of togetherness. They get caught; the growing process stops; they join the modern herd, denying their true destiny; they use busyness as a substitute for creativity; they rush from group to group, feeling guilty if they don't—feeling more and more lonely, desolate and distraught if they do.

For a person who has once been awakened but then surrenders and becomes part of the herd, the results can be even more serious than if he had never made a beginning. He may, for example, grow judgmental, with a constant need to condemn— or hard and brittle, arrogant and insensitive. He becomes closed to life, to self-awareness, to responsiveness.

In Part IV we will try to outline a process of growth that will never end, either in this or the next dimension. Those of you who can follow it are a company. While you may sometimes feel a sense of aloneness, you will not be lonely; and the wonderful fact is you will not be peculiar; you will be you, the real you, this that is the crowning achievement of all creation.

## THERE ARE MANY IN BONDS

There are many who are imprisoned; many are in bonds, sick in mind and body; many are full of rage, expressing this rage in countless ways, sometimes actually under the guise of kindness.

These, the imprisoned, the unborn, the unawakened, are incapable of enthusiasm. They are lost in the sense that on the surface of the mind they do not care. They have lost their dream power and they are chained. They have lost their capacity to look up. They are in hell, for no more do their spirits seek wings.

There are others who dream, who aspire, who have profound intent but yet are not led to act. They may be impulse-governed. They are victims of their feelings. They are always going to do things. They have great plans, but dreams alone never lead to action.

There are others akin to these, who have been so dominated from early babyhood that they are completely dependent for motivation on a concerned person. In the moment of inspiration, they are all organized to go; but when the stimulus is absent, the will is too weak to order a program of living, so that the intent does not lead to action. Others are dependent but resist authority while seeking it, usually biting the hand that feeds them.

Others are in bondage to some such tyranny as an overwhelming fear, a feeling of anxiety, an appetite like the craving for liquor, a need to prove their manhood or womanhood, a habit-driven reliance on some form of sedation.

These who are fearful, anxious or full of rage usually infect others. Often they are found in hate groups, the announced purpose of which is to oppose but which end up destroying the community, crucifying those who are true to the truth as they see it. The triumph of fear and hate can be seen in the person ready to shoot a neighbor who tries to enter his fallout shelter. Could it be that a death wish, often so dominant in the deep self, is at the heart of the modern human condition? Is it possible that persons now are so fascinated with the face of death that they have lost their power to choose life and meet the requirements for its fulfillment? Could this be why nations are in a crisis, out of which they do not know how to negotiate themselves, caught in a momentum of greed plus an habitual reliance on force that is beyond their capacity to change?

There are, of course, millions of persons in bondage to the past who want to grow and who are ready to begin if the right approach is made. Moreover, they can move on from a true start and continue becoming persons who bear the likeness of the God-image; persons who are alive; persons who are *aware* as individuals: aware of those near them; aware of persons they cannot see; aware of the suffering masses of the world; aware even of the people in the next dimension.

Irving Stone, the famous writer, once said of his mother: *"She loved me. This was for me one certain fact in an otherwise dubious world."* His family was poor and his mother had no formal education. One day she packed a lunch and took him to the University of California where they ventured onto the campus and walked all over, both of them stirred and moved by the experience. Finally, when they sat down to eat their simple meal, she looked at him and said, "My son, I may not be here to see you do it, but one thing I want you to promise me—that you'll come to this school, that you'll graduate from it, and nothing will keep you from it. You may have to do it on your own, but this is one thing I ask of you."

Mr. Stone reports that her hopes became for him a profound thrust.

In due time he reached the campus as a freshman. Toward the end of his first day he saw a man riding down over the hill on a horse. He thought it was an apparition. When finally the man came to where he was, looked down on him and said, "Young man, I want you to do your very best. If you do, the whole world will respond." Then the man road on across the campus. Later Irving Stone was told that the rider was the President Emeritus of the University.[1] That experience provided for him another thrust, one that became a guiding torch.

It was natural that the young Stone should respond to these thrusts. He was headed in the right direction from birth. He could not fail.

But others find themselves in bonds such as we have described. What, then, creates an awakening? Often it is a similar thrust. Some experience or influence breaks through the shell and the person moves out of prison into freedom. He makes a beginning. This for him is his supreme hour.

What is the source of such a thrust? It is God. His grace is infinite; He never gives us up; He is ever seeking to be known to us. He has made us free to respond or to resist. The response can be out of fear, which is a low motive, or it can be out of respect for the very law of life.

## SOME ILLUSTRATIONS

I worked on a man for years trying to get him to join with his wife creatively in our spiritual laboratory. One Sunday when there was a deep snow and only a few came to our early service they arrived. For years he had outdone me with his clever repartee. As he and his wife entered the sanctuary he asked, "Where are all your Christians?"

"They are saved so they didn't need to come. But you, not knowing who you are, had no other choice," I answered smiling. He smiled and followed his wife to a seat.

I asked the few present to gather in the choir seats, where we sang some hymns. When I asked each to give a Scripture verse he said, "Jesus wept." When I asked for sentence prayers, he was silent. Then I said to them, "Let each one say where he is in his own spiritual growth." When my friend's turn came, he began to "wisecrack"; in the middle he suddenly shifted and said, "I never felt like this inside before," and he went on and said some wonderful things. He became a devoted searcher for a spiritual way of life. He felt God's thrust and, in the reality of it, made a profound beginning.

A college student, the eldest child in his family, grew up withdrawn. Robbed of the chance for normal interaction as a baby, he grew into adolescence unable to make adjustments to others. Even the Hi-Y Club rejected him.

His I.Q. was high, but he was too busy with his many private sideline interests to study. Although he spent most of his time alone, he was not unhappy; he had wide interests covering many creative activities. He learned to live with himself, doing what he wanted to do when he wanted, and therefore found it very difficult to respond to a regular schedule, an outlined plan of study in school. He did have yearnings to be with people, but he accommodated himself remarkably well to his unpopularity.

The boy finally entered college and here began to move out into groups and even received a bid by a fraternity. But he only did average work in his classes, just getting by.

One evening his father drove to the college to have dinner with him. They ate and later drove to the bank of a stream that ran by the college campus to talk. Finally the father said, "I must leave."

The boy said to him, "Aren't you going to ask about my grades?"

The father said, "No."

"Aren't you interested?"

"Yes."

"Well, why don't you ask me?"

"It is your affair."

"You are helping me through school."

"Yes, but nevertheless your grades are your business. If you want to tell me, fine—if not, I accept it."

The boy didn't tell his father.

The very next day a great doctor and a great soul spoke in the college chapel. Suddenly this young man became alive; he was so inspired he decided he was going to be a missionary doctor. The interesting thing is, he finished two years of college in one year and came through medical school sixth in a class of eighty.

What led to his beginnings? Somewhere between the influence of the speaker and of his father, who finally gave him the feeling that his life was his own, came a thrust that impelled him to make a profound beginning. Today he is a brilliant and creative physician.

For a number of years I worked with a man who was under the tyranny of alcoholism. I did not pursue him, but now and then I would have lunch with him. When I approached someone with a problem, I always got permission to enter into his problem, otherwise I would infringe on his rights; otherwise I could easily be injuriously coercive.

His wife had come to me many times for advice but always warned, "Never tell him I've talked to you."

The first time I said to him, "Do I have your permission to talk to you about something that's entirely your business?"

He asked, "Did my wife talk to you?"

My answer was, "Is this really the question you want to ask me?"

He said, "Yes."

I said, "Well, I want to ask you again, is this really the question you want to ask me?"

I kept repeating my answer till finally he smiled and said, "You're playing games with me."

I said, "Do you really feel I'm playing games with you or do you feel that I'm interested in just being a real friend to you?"

He said, "Well, if she did talk to you I could understand it. She is very troubled about my drinking and she will not believe me when I say I can stop anytime I make up my mind to."

I never gave him a pep talk, I didn't threaten him, I didn't challenge him, I just listened to him. It has always been my feeling that if I can get a man talking, he will sometimes talk himself into the right course or will get ready to do something about his life.

But this man would say again and again, "I can stop anytime I wish." Then he would lead me away from his problem with alcohol and we would talk of other matters. We came to be close friends and had a good relationship. Finally I reached the point where I could say to him on one occasion, "If you ever are ready to do something about your drinking, let me know." And while I did not say to him that I had no intention to pursue him further, this was my decision.

From time to time his wife expressed great anxiety about his condition, feeling that sooner or later he would have an accident with his car or would lose his position, which was a very good one with a large corporation. I listened to her, upheld or sustained her when I could and simply urged her along lines like this: "I think the only thing you can do is to accept him as he is, see him as he can be, and then be led, for if you work too hard on him, if you get impatient, if you threaten him, if you make a scene, I think you will drive him further into his tyranny."

One day she said, "I can't put up with it any longer. I'm going to leave him."

I said to her, "You feel that this is the solution you want."

She left me determined to bring an end to their relationship. But she never brought herself to that point. Again and again her feelings would build up until she could bear them no longer. Then she would return, always urging me not to tell him she had been there.

One Sunday morning she came to see me with her son. She declared that she could not go on any longer. The son made a proposal to me in these words: "I have always stood by Dad, I've never been critical of him, but I've decided that I'm going to try shock treatment on him. This afternoon I'm going to say to him, 'You're an old drunk—I don't want anything to do with you. If you have an ounce of sense, you'll leave mother and support her adequately. She's had enough of your behavior.' "

I said to him, "Suppose this works the other way, suppose it injures his ego even more?"

The mother then supported her son, saying, "We have tried everything else—we want to try this, only tonight I want you to come by. Don't tell him that we have talked to you." I agreed to come when I was through with my meetings.

That Sunday night I went. As I entered he came to me and said, "I'm now ready to do something about my drinking. I have never been ready before. I've always told you that I could stop when I wanted to, but, frankly, I've found that this is not true. Now I really want to begin."

I listened to him. I wanted to hear him talk more and then he said, "I had a real shock this afternoon. You know our only son; he is married and they have three wonderful children and I adore those children. My son has always been very kind, very understanding. He's had a degree of independence, he's doing very well vocationally, but he's always been understanding. He never entered into my life, he never made judgments of me. But this afternoon he came over and sat down and looked at me for a long time. I never saw him look like that. Then he said, 'Well, all I can say to you is, I'm through with you. You're no longer my father. I have completely lost respect for you. In fact, all you are is an old drunk.' He went and kissed my wife, his mother, and then left.

"It was a big blow. It crushed me, even though in my own heart I knew I had it coming to me. Now I want to do something about my life."

He went on further to say, "I've known a number of people in Alcoholics Anonymous who wanted me to join, but I've always been too proud. I've had a number of those who are now sober say that they never could have done it without the power of prayer. You know, I've been a member of our church, but I just have never really belonged. It's never meant much; *you* know that. I tried to help in some things, but membership for me was just something I did for the same reason I've always been a Republican. I haven't worked at it."

I said, "Well, if you've learned from those who have achieved sobriety that the only way is to find prayer power, that the only way is to find strength from God in prayer, maybe you are ready to pray."

He said, "I don't know how to pray."

"You know how to talk," I pointed out. "Why don't you start talking? Prayer is opening your very being to God. Others have done this and got results. Why don't you try?"

Kneeling, he began to open his soul to God. In the middle of his prayer he suddenly opened his eyes, looked up at me in surprise, and said, "I can't explain it, but something has happened inside of me. I never felt like this."

Later he asked me if I could get someone to take him and his wife to a meeting of Alcoholics Anonymous that met in our church building. I went to the phone and called a man who had achieved sobriety. I asked him if he and his wife would stop and pick up this man and his wife on Monday night and take them to an Alcoholics Anonymous meeting.

That was a number of years ago and to this day our friend has maintained his sobriety. He knows, like many others, that he is just one drink from being a drunk, but he has kept his freedom. He is continuing in Alcoholics Anonymous and is not only a member of our church, but, in a deep sense, *belongs*.

What was the beginning? Was it not a thrust that came through his son?

A woman was rejected by her husband, who took their child from her by court order. She had emotional difficulty that finally led her into a psychotic state. One day I went into the sanctuary of our church and found her sitting there in her bathrobe. I talked to her but she didn't hear or notice me. She got up and started walking. Outside, I tried to persuade her to get into my car. She walked several blocks while I drove along the curb, trying to break through, to get her to hear. When I found it was impossible, I asked the police to take her to the state hospital for confinement and therapy.

There she entered a period of treatment. She was diagnosed as a paranoid schizophrenic with obsessional and depressive components. She began to respond a little to treatment. I went to the hospital repeatedly to see her and she held onto me as a child would to her father.

One day it occurred to me that the right woman could help her more than I, and I asked a strong and warm member of our church to visit her. The relationship between the two women became one of profound meaning to them both. They met totally. For the first time this young woman met another woman whose womanhood came through to her and whose friendship actually gave her a new sense of being. Today the woman is free, on the way to becoming whole. She is now so well that the court has granted her custody of her daughter.

If you were to talk with this woman, she would say that the turning point came for her in her relationship with the woman who visited her. For the first time she felt a close and genuine relationship with a woman. She had grown up without a mother, and she and her father were never close. The coming of this woman provided the thrust that led to a beginning toward a whole new feeling about herself.

When she was released from the hospital, she joined a research group in our spiritual laboratory where she is finding greater security as a woman and a mother.

## CONCLUSION

We have sought in this chapter to throw some light on the various bonds in which persons find themselves. We have already seen the influence of a creative fellowship, of a "radar star," and how a thrust can initiate a beginning. We go on to discover further ways in which beginnings can take place.

# CHAPTER 6. WHEN SYMPTOMS ARE *UNDERSTOOD*

There are times when a person comes to see that symptoms are deceptive, that the cause lies deeper. When this becomes clear, when the person is free to see and comprehend this, he often can make a real beginning.

Let us look at a number of situations that not only make this clear, but may be helpful to those who find it difficult to make a beginning.

## THE FIRST-BORN'S NIGHTMARES

In one of our workshops a man and woman felt compelled to keep talking about their oldest son, a boy of seven, who continually had nightmares. No matter what was suggested as possibly helpful in their difficulty, they gave the same answer: "We tried that." Yet they seemed compelled to keep talking, and other members were deprived of a chance to air their problems. Finally the leader of the workshop asked, "Would you be willing to let us go on to another experience if one of us promises to come to your home some evening, observe the child and then talk it over with you?"

They agreed, and I was appointed to the task.

When I went to see them, I arrived late in the evening but in time to see the child. It was obvious that the boy was the first-born. The first-born has a tendency to withdraw into himself; feelings for him run deep. The second-born usually achieves his place with others more readily, and he is as a rule more open, more outgoing. The third child is often a "born diplomat"—handling people for his own purposes and usually in a way that they like. For those who follow in the sequence,

53

it becomes more difficult to predict.

The first-born usually experiences more tension in his mother's body. This is, after all, her first experience. Moreover, in the beginning he is the center of attention. When the second comes along, he suddenly must share this attention and this may drive him into himself.

When I arrived that night, the child in question asked me to help put him to bed. The fellowship was good. The parents handled the situation very well.

In due time we returned to the living room. They again began to belabor the problem of the nightmares. They were obsessed with it. They kept saying the same things over and over again, always responding to suggestions with the pet phrase, "We've tried that."

Finally I asked, "Do I have your permission to ask a personal question?"

They exchanged a long look and then said hesitantly, "Well, sure."

"May I ask how you two are getting along?" I asked softly. There was a moment of heavy silence. Finally the wife burst into tears and began to pour out her dissatisfaction.

Her husband was away five days a week, leaving her alone with the children. When he returned home on Friday evening, she was eager to talk, but he was preoccupied. The children were eager to see him, but he turned away from them to his mail. During dinner when the children wanted to talk, he told them to concentrate on their meal. When she tried to make conversation, he said, "Don't bother me." After dinner he read the paper, after which he curled up on the davenport and went to sleep. She was left to do the dishes and put the children to bed. By the time she got to the living room, he would wake up and insist on going to bed. He would then use her body and soon roll over and begin to breathe heavily. She would lay awake feeling rejected, resentment mounting within her.

Saturday, when she would try to talk to him, he would become impatient and often leave for an afternoon at the office.

She was neither the type to have an affair nor a nervous break-down. Instead, she vented her feelings on the children, with the first-born suffering the most. His nightmares were the result.

As she blurted out her distress and her feelings of rejection, the young husband got very defensive. "I make the living," he said. "I've provided a nice home, and that is *my* job. *Her* job is to look after the children and be in charge of the home. But she can't be satisfied. The more I make, the more I give her, the more dissatisfied she becomes. I'm really ready to call it quits."

"You feel that to earn the money which provides for the necessities of living is your whole function?" I asked.

"Yes, I do," he came back. "I don't go out with other women, I don't play golf, I rarely drink, and I seldom buy new clothes. Smoking is the only indulgence I have."

"And Mary's job is to manage the home, look after the physical and spiritual needs of the children, be a mother and father both to them while you're away, and satisfy your biological needs?"

"That's any wife's job in my book. That's the way it was in our home, and my brother and sisters didn't have nightmares. My father would be away for two to six weeks at a time, and I never once heard my mother complain. She prized every chance moment she had with Dad."

"Jim, were you close to your father?" continued the interrogation.

"I admired him."

"You did things with him, you could go to him with anything that troubled you?"

"Well, no," Jim admitted ruefully. "My grandparents lived with us, though, and Grandpa and I were close."

"Really, then, he was your father?"

"I never thought of it in those terms," he said, the heat gone from his tone, "but I guess you're right."

"Since no grandfather is here and no other man is here, who is to be father to your three children if you are not?"

"Well, I'm here from Friday night to Monday morning."

"You're here in body," Mary chimed in, "but you're really a million miles away. Half the time they talk to you, you don't even hear them. Jim, I'm sorry to have hurt you, but do you realize how many times I talk to you that you look right through me and never hear a word I say?"

Jim continued to defend himself, but his rancor was spent. "The trouble is, dear, that you want to talk all the time. I've been away all week, talking day after day to sell my products. When I get home, you meet me at the door with a long list of troubles and right away I feel guilty that I'm away so much. When I get home I'd like to rest and relax. You expect me to be alert, alive, full of talk, and concentrate on the kids before and after dinner. Then you want *me* to put them to bed. After this, you want more talk, but I am talked out. I've run dry. I don't sleep with other women. When I get home I want to get a little loving and then go to sleep."

"Jim, that's just it. You want what you want for you. Do you have any idea what it would mean to me if you made me feel that I was a person, that I was important to you, that you wanted *me* rather than just my body? If you really wanted me, Jim, how joyfully I would give myself to you."

"I'm beginning to see your point," Jim said, seeing *her*, too, as he looked at her now. "I don't know when we talked like this. Usually you seem to put me in the doghouse, and before I know it, I'm barking at you."

"Jim, I don't want to put you there," Mary said earnestly. "You are my husband and if you could just talk to me as we are now, I'd be understanding, truly, and I wouldn't be so demanding and nagging."

"Dr. B.," said Jim, turning to me, "when you first asked how we were getting along, I immediately got resentful. I felt you were here to help us with Bob, not to pry into our affairs. Are you trying to tell us that the nightmares are my fault?" I refrained from comment, and he went on to answer his own question. "Well, I guess what happens is that Mary puts me in the doghouse, or I put myself there; then I growl my way through the week-end and then take off. Mary feels frustrated and lonely and takes it out on the children. Bob gets tense and has his nightmares and everyone loses sleep."

"That's the way it seems to sum up to me," I agreed.

The last vestige of Jim's reserve and hostility crumbled: "Mary," he said, reaching for her hand, "really I do want to be a good husband. I should be glad you want more of me. I think my mother got to the point where she learned to get along without Dad. Deep down I wouldn't want this. I've been expecting you to do all the giving. You're right. I have to give a little, too—and more than cash."

Mary kissed him right then and there. "I couldn't ask for more," she said happily.

"Mary, if I slip, call this guy in again, will you?" he said, grinning at me to hide the embarrassment inevitable at having revealed so much of himself to an outsider.

"Jim, I doubt that you'll need me or anyone else," I said. "But we might talk a little about the practical side now. Say the week-end is starting. You just got home. First you greet—really greet—Mary and the children. Then why not go upstairs, take a bath, and grab a nap. That way you'll be refreshed for spending the evening with Mary and the children. Saturday morning—not afternoon—you go to the office, read your mail and do whatever business must be done. Then the rest of the week-end belongs to Mary and the children. But not at the expense of those naps and a good night's sleep. That's where you come in, Mary." I wagged a slightly admonishing finger at her. There had to be co-operation all around. It wasn't to be all Jim's doing. "Then, occasionally, the two of you can withdraw together. Go out now and then on a Saturday night and keep most of the week-end afternoons for the kids."

"It could be so simple," Jim smiled.

I rose to go. Then something happened which really touched me.

"Dr. B.," began Jim, "would you—that is, if you don't mind

—help us say our vows again before you go?" I certainly did not mind.

When I withdrew finally, they were in each other's arms.

Jim and Mary entered a new era of their lives. Not long ago I was in a city not far from the one where they now live and they came to see me. They were radiant. I saw their children, too, including the first-born. Parents and children appeared free, alive, vital, and warm.

What was the point of beginning? They came to see that the nightmares were a *symptom;* the real issue lay in their relationship.

## A WOMAN'S ECZEMA

A woman was troubled by eczema. She went from doctor to doctor but got no help. Finally she went to a counselor. As he listened and she talked, the clearer it became to her that the eczema was a symptom of deep dissatisfaction in her own life.

She and her husband had never found a satisfying relationship. He was businesslike, very methodical. He was unromantic. She was romantic, very feminine, imaginative.

She realized that she had married her husband because he was predictable, and seemed stable. Moreover, she had been confident that he would be a great success in business. But she soon discovered that he did not know how to make love. There was nothing actually wrong with the act itself, but it never brought them truly close. They remained strangers.

As her dissatisfaction grew, she put increasing pressure on her children, and as they grew up, they drifted farther and farther away from her. She could make an impression on them only through great explosions of temper.

Finally she developed eczema. In the counseling situation she came to see ultimately that the eczema was a symptom of emotional frustration—that it was psychogenic, in other words. She came to realize that she must come to accept her husband as he was, then to see him as he could be, and try patiently to build a creative relationship with her children.

In the meantime, her counselor offered to have lunch with her husband. She agreed with the understanding that he would be very careful what he said to him.

At lunch, the husband was eager to talk about all the money he had spent to treat his wife's eczema. The counselor said, "You have willingly paid for all these treatments?"

"Indeed I have," said the man. "I'd do anything for her."

"Do you have any idea of the stress under which she lives?"

"Yes, I do. She's always fussing at the children, and every now and then she goes through periods of complaining to me that I'm not thoughtful; that I reject her; that I'm cold; that I'm overly methodical; that I'm not romantic."

"Do you feel that your wife is fair in her appraisal of you?" the counselor asked.

"Perhaps, but I am a practical man."

"That may be," the counselor acknowledged. "But there is also a quality of warmth about you, and sensitivity. Isn't it true that you are very affectionate with your children?"

"Well, I guess I am."

"Do you feel that it's inappropriate for a man's man to be affectionate and tender with his wife, too?"

The counselor struck at one of the man's shakiest defenses with this question. The air of confidence faded perceptibly. "I guess I just haven't learned how to be a lover. I make love like I go through a business deal," he said wryly.

"Maybe you are really more sensitive in business. You *are* very successful after all."

"But hardly as a husband."

"This is the way you feel?" The counselor waited while his companion stared at his plate.

"How can I change?" he asked finally. The words hadn't come easily.

"You are a wise man," said the counselor. "You can change if you want to. Wanting to is the most important step. Then you may have to act your way into a different way of feeling in order to come to that feeling."

It seemed like a big order. "How do I accomplish that?" the man wondered.

"Think for a minute," urged the counselor. "Then *you* tell *me*."

It was a struggle for such a man to imagine himself in this new role and more of an effort to picture himself thus to another man, but he began—if painfully.

"Well, I suppose one thing I could do is bring her little things, like a rose. Now and then I could bring her a box of candy. When I come home, I could put my arms around her. Oftener than I have done in the past, I could take her out for a happy evening. Up to now, I've seldom bought her presents. I've given her the money and let her do her own buying. I found her reading a book on how to make love recently. I could read it, too. Maybe I can get over to her how I really feel about her."

"It seems to me you have a good understanding of your role," the counselor told him. "After all, love involves much more than the physical to a sensitive woman like your wife; it is a relationship in which heaven and earth seem to come together; in which spirit and flesh become one and yet spirit remains spirit and flesh remains flesh. In maximum fulfillment, two persons become one. Through their closeness they become whole. Carry out your plan, embellish it, and your wife will be given the medicine she needs."

Several luncheons later, the counselor was advised that the eczema had disappeared. Two people had moved to a new level of life. What was the starting point? The discovery that the eczema was a symptom.

## A MAN'S SLEEPLESSNESS

A young minister with great skill and an attractive personality became so anxious he could not sleep. A famous evangelist came to the city where he lived. He went to him and bared his soul as to what was going on in his life. He talked about his youth and childhood, too. His father, a very successful man, had never been a real father to him. The only time the son saw him was Sunday morning and then his father criticized him, condemned him, gave him the feeling that he could never measure up.

The young man went through high school, through college, through professional school, and then got married, choosing a very outstanding wife. Everything went well until their first child came, when he began to go out with other women. He was a man of impressive personality and easily fell into the role of the conquering hero. At first, he played on the sympathies of women. He had a need to be adored. When he came near certain women who would respond, he touched them, looked deeply into their eyes, and used various verbal approaches: "It seems as if I have always known you." "I feel close to you." "To have you in the audience is a great inspiration. Tonight I felt that you and I were all by ourselves."

Finally, he became more bold. He asked one woman to meet him for lunch. At this meeting, sensing her hunger, he laid the groundwork. "I have a great wife," he said. "She is a wonderful person. I just don't love her. I'd rather be with you ten minutes than to be with her in bed a whole night." It went on from there until he went to her house when her children were in school and her husband at work.

Finally they entered a relationship of complete intimacy. At the conclusion, he was tender and rationalized that they were really married.

As she responded fully and declared her full devotion, he kept in touch, returning to her at intervals. But soon he found that this first woman was not sufficient to satisfy him. He was still restless. He longed for other women. In time, he was unfaithful with another partner.

After a woman gave in to him, she became a burden instead of an inspiration. Once she had come to him fully, he no longer needed her. She had served her purpose for him. Being unsure of his manhood, the vote of many was required.

It went on until finally he became sleepless.

He went to a doctor and got sleeping pills but could not bring himself to share his secret. He did bare his soul to the evangelist, however, who said to him, "If you give yourself to the Lord, He will forgive you and you will be free." Then they knelt together. They prayed together many times, but the young man time and again rose from his knees and went out in search of another woman.

Once when I was in the city where he and his parents lived, he came to one of my meetings with his mother. At the close he came to me and said, "As I listened to you, I felt that I had met someone who could help me." We made an appointment for ten o'clock in the evening.

For three nights I listened to him talk about his inability to sleep and about the things he had been doing and the problems that he was facing. He said, "I simply can't go on. I must find a way to sleep or I can't go on."

"You have been sleepless for a long time?"

"No, I think it started soon after we had our first child."

"You were kept awake by the child at night?"

"Oh, no. My wife always cared for the baby."

I didn't comment.

"You seemed today to be so understanding, I thought you could tell me why I can't sleep."

"You've been to a doctor?"

"Yes, I've had two complete physical examinations. I'm sound as a dollar. One doctor thought I might have an overactive thyroid. But, sorry to say, he found otherwise."

Again I was silent.

"I can't talk to my father. He does all the talking. Never listens. I've always hated him. But I can talk to you. You listen and are slow to talk."

"I need to listen to you if I'm to be helpful."

"You may wonder why I hate my father. It's not just that he won't listen. He was always away. When he *was* home, he would work me over and browbeat me, always pointing out what a great disappointment I was to him because I didn't help my mother enough and didn't do well in school."

"You feel it helps you to hate him?"

"It makes me feel better to belittle him, to rile him. I act up until he is forced to leave the room."

"You still do this?"

"No, but I delight in shocking him."

"When you can't sleep, do you dwell on your feelings toward your father?"

"Yes, sometimes I entertain fantasies of his death, feeling how great it would be if he would skid into a tree and be killed."

"You feel good about this?"

"Yes and no. Part of me feels good and part of me feels bad." Then he looked startled and asked, "You don't think that that is why I am unable to sleep?"

"If that were the cause, wouldn't it be wise to go to him and ask for a real talk? If he agrees, then tell him of your feelings and ask him to help you feel good toward him, not as a son since now you are a father yourself, but as a close man friend."

"I don't think he could take it."

"You feel you could take it?"

"By gum, he's home now with mother. I'll stay there tonight and I'll talk to him tonight or early in the morning."

He then hesitated for a number of seconds, and finally came out with: "If you think that being angry at my father might cause me not to sleep, I wonder what you would think of other things." He went on to confess what I have already described, his life with a number of women. When he had finished, he added, "I don't see how that could cause my sleeplessness, though. If I don't have a woman, I'm nervous and restless. I haven't been a husband to my wife since she got pregnant with our third one. I'm impotent with her. And if I don't make love to a woman at least every other night, I get tense. When I do, I feel peace. You may think I should be ashamed, but I believe God understands."

"God may understand, but is He pleased at your way of life? Does it not violate His laws and the laws of man? Can you really feel genuine? What would happen if this information became generally known?"

"I would be through," he said quickly. "Do you think I'm a psychopath?" he added.

"You have a reason for asking this?"

"Well, I thought you would think so when I told you I felt no guilt or shame."

"I wonder if you would hesitate to tell me if you were completely without these feelings."

"You think I am a phony, don't you?" he demanded.

"I really don't see how you can feel yourself to be genuine," I replied. "You have a number of women serving your need. Not one knows about the others. You are fooling your wife, you are fooling each woman, and you are fooling yourself. On the conscious level you achieve peace from these adventures. But are you at peace deep down? Or are you avoiding your conscience by keeping very busy?"

"You do think I'm a phony," he persisted.

"I wouldn't use that word," I said, "but you *are* acting a lie over and over again. I read a story recently about a young man who had a chance to make $10,000 by just a little cheating. When he told his mother about it, she said, 'Son, I'd hate to come to call you in the morning and find you awake.' "

"You think my generally messed-up life causes me to be sleepless?"

"It's not for me to say."

"Let's call it quits for tonight. Will you pray with me?"

"I'd like you to pray first."

"Why?"

"Paul said, 'Outdo one another in showing honor.' "

"You said in one of your articles that you are slow to pray for others, lest you drive their feelings underground."

"Then you know already why I want you to pray."

"Dear Lord, help me stay away from women," he began.

"You are facing in the wrong direction," I interrupted. "Which way do you want to go?"

"What do you mean?"

"What do you really want?"

"I want to sleep."

"Do you want your wife really to be your wife?"

"I should want that. But I'm not going home tonight anyway. I'm going to stay to talk with Dad."

We talked a bit more, but he left without further prayer.

He returned the following two nights, but made no reference to any talk he may have had with his father.

I listened to him for six or seven hours more. He talked of how he had grown up without a father—there had been one, of course, but he had been less of a "father" to him than his mother had been. He realized that he had come to depend on his wife as he had on his mother, content only if she praised him continually and tended his every need. The result was that he transferred his mother-feeling to his wife. Then his children became competitors. Deep within him he had a profound fear that he was homosexual, which impelled him to go from woman to woman to prove his manhood. Each time he was able to fulfill a woman affirmed his manhood—for the time being.

At our last meeting he said, "Every time the evangelist prayed with me, I sought some woman right afterward. The last two nights I did not go to a woman, but I could tonight."

"If you do go out and fail again, remember you've a right to fail because you're not God. Don't go to Calvary just for yourself."

He went home and later reported to me that for the first time in his life his wife was his wife and no longer his mother.

As his wife became his wife and he became sure of his manhood, he no longer had a need to hate his father. And, amazingly enough, a friendship grew up between the two men.

He went to each woman and told her how wrong he had been; that in his need to be adored, he had used her. In each case, he asked forgiveness.

That is now almost two years ago. He has not slipped once. Today he can sleep. Today he is free. Now he knows that his sleeplessness was a symptom.

Everything that happened with the evangelist was valid. The only trouble was that the sleepless man was not free to respond at the time. He first needed to understand the situation. He needed to see the nature of his bonds and seeing this, he found the strength to build a bridge between the intent and the act. Then he became free; he became whole.

The symptom finally drove him to a beginning and to deal with the real situation. Subsequently he bared his soul to his wife, and when I saw her last she said, "I have accepted it, though it was a blow. But it was harder to have him with me after our children began to come without his really being there."

## OTHER ILLUSTRATIONS

A man became bitter when his son had an illness that led to his spirit leaving his body. The bitterness he felt drove him also to unacceptable types of behavior. It continued for a long time, and finally he realized that his continued depression and bitterness over the loss of his son was a symptom of a deep problem within his own personality. This man, too, had grown up without a father. He, too, was not sure of his manhood; he also went from woman to woman. The birth of his son was only partially reassuring to him. When he lost him, he was driven into severe bitterness.

In time he came to understand the real meaning of his behavior, which gave him a point of beginning that led to the achievement of great wholeness as a man. He was now able to focus all his love on his wife, and he became a man in the real sense of the word.

Another man had a slow pulse and on occasion would faint. His doctor treated him and listened to him but was never able to diagnose his difficulty. And then something happened that threw light on it. His son stole some money from his wallet one night while he slept. To me he declared, "I'll beat that boy within an inch of his life."

"You have a right to punish him, for what he did was wrong. But, may I ask, did you ever steal?"

If I had slapped him he could not have shown more surprise. He was silent for a while. Finally he said, "When I was a boy I stole twelve dozen eggs from my mother and sold them, spending the money; now she is dead and I can never be forgiven."

"Oh, yes, you can," I told him. "When Johnny confesses to you, you can ask for forgiveness."

When he arrived home, Johnny approached him. "Dad, I did a terrible thing," he blurted. "I stole five dollars from you. Here it is. If you will forgive me, I'll never do it again."

"Johnny, what you did was very wrong. But when I was a boy, I stole twelve dozen eggs from my mother and sold them and spent the money. I thought that I never could be forgiven, but tonight I learned that when I forgive you, I, too, can be forgiven."

"We learned in church school that if *you* forgive people, God will forgive you," Johnny remembered.

The father hugged his son. He has not fainted since and that is now eleven years ago.

So we could go on, endlessly almost, describing situations where symptoms, when once understood, become points of beginning.

## CONCLUSION

Perhaps most of us have understood at some time that people can cling to symptoms rather than face the real source of their problems. But it is not so easy to see when we ourselves are doing this. When we can discover ourselves doing this, and why, we can make valid beginnings toward the achievement of wholeness.

There are two things we need to say which have been already implied: beginnings are basic. But they are no guarantee that one will move on toward solutions in an ongoing search. Beginnings actually can be substitutes for ongoingness. Many people make beginnings; they make resolutions but stop there.

In many cases, the beginnings can be false starts. They can take place as the result of an emotional stimulus and lose their power when the stimulus is lost. Thus the person is free to start, but not to go on.

The "sleepless" man went to a well-known evangelist, as we pointed out, confessed to him, and asked for prayer. The evangelist prayed for him and then said, "Give yourself to Christ and you will be free." Whereupon the young man rose and left to go to one of the women whose major function was to give him proof that he was a man.

The other word needs to be said for the benefit of those who are working with people. There are those who will not make a beginning. They cannot be reached until time runs out. We look into this carefully in Chapter 8. Jesus himself was not always successful. The rich young ruler made no beginning. Judas did, but he got off on a tragic detour.

A real principle for the leader is to realize that the mark of success is not immediate progress but faithfulness. Each person must make his own beginning. This is important to realize in terms of all living relationships, not simply counseling ones. A person can only be helped when he is ready. Pressure can, in fact, intensify his bonds. The best anyone can do for another is to see him as he is, as he can be, and listen—in the hope that the person will find his own impetus to begin.

# CHAPTER 7.  WHEN THE SHOCK OF SHAME IS FELT

Many people are swept along by an inner tyranny until they find themselves morally in a dead-end street. They are then exposed; their problem is no longer hidden; they can no longer escape. In such situations I have seen persons make a beginning. The crisis became a shock treatment; they were jarred. They not only got ready for a new start but moved on to greatness in character and usefulness.

But such a change does not always occur. I have seen alcoholics reach crises, for example. I have heard them vow to change and yet they remained under tyranny. I have seen such failures in various forms of what might be called addiction. I have known homosexuals, for example, who were apprehended, penalized, and ultimately released. I have heard them vow they would never do it again. When they have allayed the fears of those who know them best and their own fear of apprehension has been quieted, they often repeat their behavior.

Nevertheless, when the shock of shame comes and the problem is brought out into the open, often a new beginning takes place. The beginning often involves health-making forces which do not appear on the surface.

## THE DRIVING FORCE OF GUILT

Most persons, unless they are sociopaths, are beset by guilt when they engage in wrongdoing. Guilt may make the person sick or impel him to project it onto others. Moreover, it seems to drive the person to keep on doing the very thing that created the guilt in the first place.

But it goes deeper than this. When a person breaks the laws

of life, he moves into a strange apartness. He becomes an illusion of a person. In a deep sense, he is a "phoney." Professor Ross Snyder, commenting on the hard-driving words of Dr. O. Hobart Mowrer of the University of Illinois, who feels that the Freudian influence in America deals with guilt feelings but not with guilt and thus undermines the moral basis of our society, expressed dynamically some thoughts which I have his permission to use.[1]

Dr. Mowrer's thrust is this—guilt is the major trouble with man. If so, then a new kind of therapy, church life, and ministerial behavior is called for.

Guilt, if rooted in actual wrongdoing, results in a separation from people, because such wrongdoing violates the moral and communal nature of man. Then fear is loosed that you will be found out and unveiled before persons you respect, so you erect defenses and enter upon a life of duplicity—seeming to be to others and yourself what you know deep-down you are not. So you destroy the possibility of authentic communication and engage instead in prattle. Your recurring taste of yourself is as gall. You lose your freedom; you become wrapped up in yourself—your guilt having become your jailer. You become afflicted with the "over-the-shoulder tic"—the head jerking and turning to catch if someone's eyes are boring into you and observing your secret. Your life becomes devoid of love, and you can trust no one fully. You are in hell.

So the trouble with people is not so much that they have harnessed the id, but repressed the conscience. Not simply "guilt feelings," but real guilt exists. No man has been destroyed because he has experienced injustice or because he has had to recognize that he is different from other people; but he can be destroyed by breaking with authenticity. His hope lies in his naturalization papers as a citizen of the land of nonduplicity.

As Dr. Boisen pointed out years ago, man can recover if he takes responsibility for what he has done, rather than putting the blame on parents or society or the times; if he retains the power to see and judge himself as he really is; and if he continues to suffer because of what he sees. Two more acts enable the rescue—confession and pouring something back into life to heal life's wounds, bridge its chasms, fill its wastelands.

## DEALING WITH GUILT

Guilt must be dealt with or it will have serious consequences, if no more than to dull a person's capacity to reform, to make him more and more a victim. Anyone can violate the laws of life but one thing he cannot do: he cannot choose the consequences. These he must live with. Whatever a man sows, this shall he reap.

But how can a person deal with guilt? In the steps that follow we will try to point up some principles that I have found to be basic.

First, the person must see his wrong. He does see and feel this to a degree unless he is a sociopath, but he goes on—perhaps rationalizing it. He can carry on in his wrong until he feels little pain on the conscious level. But he loses his alertness or he becomes overactive: he may drink, or indulge in excesses in work, play, or social activity as a way of running from himself. So, while at first he felt troubled, he is driven on perhaps by the guilt that he felt in the beginning. His wrongdoing becomes compulsive.

He therefore must recover the freedom to see his wrong. The shock of shame, the feeling that his separation from others and himself is now consciously shared by those who mean most to him, can have great meaning. He can no longer run; no longer can he take on one role with some while with others he pretends to be something else. He faces himself squarely. This is the first step.

Second, he may need to face with a trusted person or an intimate group the wrong he has done. He can no longer run from his guilt; he must face it and deal with it. If he shares with a trusted friend, a priest, or a group and is accepted, he will move toward healing. There are of course those who work this out in their own meditative life.

Third, if he chooses to share his problems, the group needs

then to accept him, not condoning the wrong he did, but accepting *him*. Before them he takes full responsibility for his wrong. Whatever judgments they make must never be characterized by condemnation but born of compassion and understanding.

Fourth, they accept him now as he is and as he can be. They assure him of forgiveness by God, for the Bible gives us abundant assurance of pardon.

Fifth, he needs to seek the help that will enable him to discover the roots to the behavior which robbed him of authenticity as a person. In the stories that follow there will be suggestions along this line.

Sixth, the final step involves his moving beyond words to action. With prayer power he begins to live the new life that keeps him in harmony with the laws of wholeness. He ministers to others not to atone but because now he is a part of humanity. He is moving out of hell into heaven in this life. He ministers with helpfulness because he is fully alive himself.

Once he was related to those who were a part of what was wrong with him. Now he has found relationships with those who are representative of what is right with him. Having been ministered unto, he now ministers.

## WHEN A DICTATOR INCREASED HIS PRESSURE

A president of a company, a man who habitually used harsh dictatorial tactics, found himself in a profound crisis.

One of his vice-presidents was in charge of personnel. He was very successful, earned a high salary, and was loved by all members of the organization—all, that is, except the president, who browbeat him. The boss worked over the executives on his staff by turns. He was most ruthless with those who were unable to hide their distress. Their discomfort gave him a heightened sense of his own power. The vice-president in charge of personnel suffered the most at the hand of the president because he was loved by the staff.

Some would fight back, many would leave. The turnover in the company was high. The boss took every opportunity to downgrade to other employers those who resigned. This personnel director didn't fight back. He suffered in silence. He never discussed his boss with anyone, not even his wife, though she knew when he came home that the day had been hard, and others revealed to her the tactics of the president.

This vice-president had a fatal heart attack, and his wife found herself in what seemed to be an unresolvable state of resentment. She would say to me, "Many a woman loses her husband to another woman; I lost mine to the hostility of his boss."

The boss attended the Service of Memory I held for his employee. Prior to the beginning of the service he shook hands with the young widow. I was by her side at the time. When he said, "I am so sorry," she lifted her head, looked him in the eyes and said, "I wish I could believe you. I think you, with your regular diet of browbeating, killed George." The boss was stunned; he became white as a sheet; his lips quivered but no words came. Finally he turned, walked to a pew, and sat down to wait for the service to begin.

The ceremony was simple. I began by talking with the people about the man—what his family said about him, what our church people felt, what many of his fellow workers felt. I pointed out that he knew to a great degree who he was; that his understanding of himself led others to new understanding; that he was so kind that those who came in contact with him were often inspired to emulate him. But some place along the line he may not have found out how to avoid the pressures that used up so quickly his physical reserves.

One day the employer's wife came to see me. "I had to talk to you," she began. "We don't belong to your church, but I came to you because I am concerned about my husband. He's in a daze. He's utterly desolate. He has always been too busy and difficult to live with. He has a need to prove himself.

"You know who his father is and how successful he is. He gave my husband everything but himself. My husband could never measure up. He always fell short of what his father expected. His father delighted in belittling him in public.

"When my husband graduated from Harvard Business School, he came back and was made vice-president in his dad's company. We'd been married while he was still in school and were living in Cambridge. When we came home we moved into a large house which had been built for us and fully furnished. This hurt us, but we had to act as though we loved it.

"My husband received a large salary, but his father never respected him. It was intolerable. One day, to my joy, he came home and said, 'I resigned, and I'm going to start my own business.'

" 'I'm so glad,' I told him. 'I'll do anything. I'd take in washing to help you.'

"In the beginning the going was rough. My husband made great demands on himself and on everyone. He paid good salaries but he put himself and everyone else under great pressure. We at home felt it but we held on.

"But now he is beside himself—ever since George died. Last night he kept talking about him and his funeral. I suggested that he go to see you. He got up without a word and went out and didn't come in until two o'clock this morning. I was afraid to ask if he'd seen you. But I figured he would have told me if he had. I can see that he hasn't. Could you, *would* you, call him?"

"Maybe at our service club I'll see him," I said. "It would be better if he initiated the relationship."

We did run into one another in due time, and he seemed eager to talk. I suggested that he come to my office. He said that he would rather see me in his office, that his secretary would serve us lunch. We met quite regularly at first and then infrequently over a period of three years. After the first year, he came to me.

At our first meeting, he was visibly shaken. In fact, his wife had been right, he was desolate.

"I killed George as truly as if I had shot him," he declared.

"I didn't give it a thought until his wife exploded to me before the service. That stunned me. When I recovered myself a little, I began to resent her. George was the best-paid man in his field in the city, maybe in the country. But it's true, I did work him over regularly, sometimes beyond reason. Feelings would build up in me and I'd take it out on the men. I guess I always had someone on the carpet.

"But others got mad. They would fight back or leave. George never did. He never even showed resentment. In fact, he used to infuriate me. He would even show me some special kindness. He is the last one who should have had a heart attack. He was so mature; so self-possessed.

"The other day I overheard two men talking in the office. One said, 'George was so patient. He had more damn good-will than any man I know. When the chief (that's what they call me) would jump on him, he never talked back.'

"'Yes, he did,' the other one said, 'he talked back with a coronary.'

"First there was his wife's denunciation of me, and then this. That did it. I'm at the end of my rope. But it's not just that I'm a murderer. I've been pushing people around for years, even my family. I haven't even been honest. To get contracts, I'd stop at nothing: get the prospects drunk, furnish women for them; I even buy them for myself when I'm out of town. It makes me sick now to look back on what I've been, what I've done. I've made life miserable for my wife. Sometimes she'd fight back, but then she'd forgive me. She got a terrible deal. I've used her, but never had any time for her. I've always been under pressure; we've never been really close. I'd missed her when I was away, but I'd fill the void by paying a fee to a woman. I knew it was wrong, but I kept rationalizing. Now life has caught up with me. My wife looks at me so strangely, and I feel that my employees are on the one hand condemning me and, on the other, feeling sorry for me.

"You are not my minister, but I have no relationship with ours. When I've gone to church my mind's been so full, I haven't heard him. Your service for George made me feel I could talk with you. Besides, you knew and loved George. Do you think there's any hope for me? For the past few days I've been thinking of going out in my car and driving as fast as I can into a tree."

There was a pause. "Well, I must say, you're at least a good listener," he remarked. "Now that you know what a mess I've made of things, can you honestly say there's any hope for me?"

"Of course there is hope."

This is what he wanted to hear, but he couldn't believe it. He had a need to be harsh with himself.

"You have bared your soul," I pointed out. "You have trusted me enough to tell me some things you have kept secret, and you are facing the implications of George's fatal coronary."

"You don't think less of me?"

"I think more highly of you. You are facing the wrong you have done. You have not shifted the blame. You look squarely at yourself and you assume full responsibility."

"At least I ought to be man enough for that."

"You are man enough."

"My wife hates my father," he said suddenly, "or rather she resents him. She feels that he never respected me."

"This is your feeling, too."

"Well, I am not going to blame my father. What has happened is my responsibility."

"Good."

"But I do think I had to make good at least to prove to myself that I am worthy to be his son."

"Or, worthy to be you."

"What do you mean?"

"You are a husband and father, so it is not easy for you to be a son, too. Maybe in time you and your father can become close friends."

"He is proud of me now. I haven't told my wife yet, but my father bought a ten per cent interest in my company from another man, saying it was the best investment he ever made. He's now a member of my Board of Directors. He gave me 5,000 shares in his company some years ago. When I started my company, I sold them. Recently I bought them back and I'm on his Board of Directors."

"You really want to keep this from your wife?"

"Yes, for a little while longer."

"You no longer need to prove yourself."

"I never thought of it in that way."

We were now off to a good start. As time went on he needed to deal with his guilt.

"I am a murderer and there is no forgiveness for me," he repeated.

"Jesus prayed on the cross, 'Father, forgive them for they know not what they do.'"

"But I knew, at least to a degree."

"Yes, that's true. But if George were to talk to us, I don't believe he would blame you. He might say instead 'I should have learned to talk back rather than bottle up my feelings.' Besides, George was a heavy smoker and he played hard and ate too much. I played golf with him once and he ate a big lunch and then went out and played eighteen holes of golf."

"But no matter what you say, I contributed to his attack. I should have shown him appreciation instead of browbeating him," said my troubled friend.

"You felt pressure and you passed it along," I said.

"What can I do?" he asked.

"What would you like to do?"

"I've thought of getting all my top employees together and baring my sins to them. But I'm afraid they may never respect me again."

"You can get them together for a real evening; let them talk about policies. If you wish you can bare your soul or you can be a new chief and they will soon catch on."

"I see what you are saying. It is one thing for me to make a statement of where I have been wrong and what I'm going to do, it is something else to be that person."

The meeting was arranged. I wanted to have him rehearse what he was going to say, but I restrained myself. He asked me to be present. I finally agreed with some misgivings.

The meeting had an air of tension. When the meal was finished, he rose to speak. It was a dramatic moment. He began, "I needed to meet with you for there are many things on my heart." He traced the growth of the company and then came to the point of the pressure he put on people and the relationship of this to George's fatal heart attack. He closed by saying simply, "I hope not only to be a team leader but a member of the team. This does not mean that I will not at times feel pressure and pass it on, for the competition today is pronounced. But I am alerted; I know better what is 'cooking' if I may use the word. I want us to have a relationship in which leaders grow, in which the best is called forth from each. To go a step further, I want a relationship in which we help each other to meet the requirements for a real team."

He sat down. There was no applause. The eighteen officers and executives and his personal secretary were moved deeply. Finally one rose to talk. His words set the stage, "Chief, for the first time I feel that you really are my chief. I deeply respect you for baring your soul to us. That took courage. I believe you may assume more than your share of the blame for George's death."

Another talked. This went on until each had spoken. Each one spoke with appreciation. His personal secretary was last. When the meeting adjourned, they swarmed about the chief, some of the men even hugged him. His secretary had tears in her eyes when she left. He later said to me that his relationship with her had vastly improved.

When the members of his team had gone, we went back to his office.

"I didn't understand it. How could they respond with such understanding?"

"They accepted the real chief. Up to this time, you were not you. Tonight the real person was revealed to them."

"I feel more like a man right now than ever in my life."

He hesitated a moment. "I must see George's wife," he said. "I must ask her forgiveness and then in time give her and her children stock in the company George helped to build."

"She will get benefits from the company insurance."

"Yes, but only half of George's salary. I'll give her enough stock to make her income equal to his salary."

"You feel you must do this?"

"I could only bear myself if I did this. Could we go right now?"

I called and asked George's widow if we could come. She agreed reluctantly.

As we entered she was sullen. Finally, she told off our friend as I have rarely heard anyone worked over. He whitened. Each word was worse than a blow in the face. Finally spent, she began to cry. I tried to comfort her. She sobbed for a long time. When she recovered, our friend said, "I deserve everything you have said. I am deeply to blame and I have no defense. I know that to ask forgivenes is a poor way to atone. I'd like to give you enough stock so that your income from insurance and the stock will equal what George made. The stock should be yours because your husband was with me from the beginning."

"I don't want your old stock. I never want to see you again," she burst out.

With this, our friend, visibly shaken, got up to leave. I told George's widow that I would see her the next day if she was willing. Then I left with the "chief."

"She is really angry," he said dismally.

"She needs to blame someone now," I said. "You were fine with her. You did well. You were a man."

"But I certainly failed with her. I feel I have lost some things I found tonight."

"You'll regain them," I promised. "George's widow is angry about more than George's going. It's coming to the surface now. She may well end up one of your good friends. She was once a secretary; her children are in school; she in time might make a good woman for your organization."

"I'm ready to do anything that will help."

"Maybe you should wait a little before transferring the stock to her."

"Now I must go home to report to Mary. Do you think I should confess my infidelity to her?"

"No, you have confessed to God and me, and you came clear in other ways to your staff. Of course, it's really up to you. Some take the course not to confess but to make up for infidelity by being a better husband; some confess. I have seen both work."

"But Mary and I could have a great marriage. I don't want to go on living with her under false colors. I want her to know the person I have been. It will hurt her, but then it will be through. If I don't clear it all up, I think she will be hurt the rest of our lives. I'm going to come clean and if she'll forgive me, I'd like you to marry us again. Then I'll have an unbroken vow."

When I arrived home, my wife had pinned a note where I could see it, a note to call George's widow.

"Oh, thank you for calling," she said when I reached her. "I feel terrible for the way I acted tonight. You must know why I have been so resentful."

"I think he understands. But you might call him tomorrow."

She chose not to wait. She got him just as he arrived home. What she said prepared him for the final act of wiping his slate clean.

His wife was crushed by the news, although she had much evidence for what she now knew as fact. And as time went on, it became more and more clear that telling her all was necessary to achieve the wholeness they now share.

The time came when they joined me to say their vows again. I am sure these will be kept not because they feel they *ought*, but because of love.

We continued to meet. He came increasingly to travel all the roads we will later follow in Part III.

What was the point of departure? A moral crisis. The crisis proved a crossroads at which he made a beginning. Today he is one of the most beloved employers in our city. He is a true leader now, for he is able to create a relationship in which leaders grow and in which the requirements for the team are met.

## A MAN WITH GREAT COMPASSION

Persons in the penitentiary have sometimes appealed to me to sponsor their parole. I have done this for many, in which effort I have had the help of an outstanding businessman who belongs to another church in our city. He was in a business in which he could give men employment. We never lost one person. Every man came through.

When I became Minister Emeritus, he called me and suggested lunch. At the conclusion of the lunch he said, "Have you ever wondered why I was eager to help you rehabilitate those prisoners?"

I said, "No, I never really did. I was just grateful to know that you were interested."

"Well," he said, "I want to tell you a story. Many years ago I worked for a company in our city. I delivered goods and collected money. Over a period of time I stole around $750. One morning early my boss showed up and said, 'You go home. I'll take your route today. Don't tell your wife why you're not working, but tonight I would like you both to come to our home. I'd like to have a visit with you.' " He paused and his expression must have reflected what he had felt in that long-ago moment. "Don't tell me there isn't a hell," he said. "I was there. And you don't have to tell me how long eternity is—I know. All day long my wife asked, 'Why are you home?' She knew I was troubled. I could only say, 'I can't tell you.' That night we went to the home of my boss. When we entered he hugged my wife and his wife hugged me. We were led to the fireplace where we sat down. After visiting a while, he turned to me and said, 'Now why don't you tell your wife why you didn't go to work?' "

What a sensitive way of handling it! The boss did not condemn him, but with compassion and understanding let him judge himself.

"I began blurting out the awful story," my friend went on. "When my wife realized what I was saying, she became hysterical, threw herself at my feet and sobbed and sobbed. When she finally got hold of herself, I finished the story.

"Then my boss took a seat and said, 'What you did was very wrong. We trusted you; you let us down. I could have you put in the penitentiary, but I'm not going to do it. I'm going to give you another chance. So come to work tomorrow. We will not let you handle money yet, for you must win the right to do this.' "

That, again, was judgment with understanding. "I went back to work," my friend continued, his eyes filling with tears, "and eleven years later I was elected president of that company."

We both sat without talking for a time, and then I said finally, "I've never heard a more beautiful story in all my life."

For him, and for the other man, a moral crisis became the stimulus for a great and true beginning.

## CONCLUSION

Many mental patients first move toward the light following electric shock treatment. But such physical shock is not necessary to start a new beginning. There is another kind of shock: one comes to the end of the road; he is either discredited or he reaches the point where his dilemma is beyond him. Then he comes to himself and often is able to make a beginning and grow to the place where he can live with himself. He may never be free from regret, but he grows in the realization that where he has been is no longer so important as where he is going. Establishing either the right relationship in a creative fellowship or finding a relationship with a trusted friend or counselor can make it possible for him to grow into wholeness and usefulness. As he accepts the past, does all possible to make restitution, then moves into the future, he will find acceptance from genuine people.

When once the person has dealt with the past, met the requirements for forgiveness, including forgiving himself, he can then focus on the future. The more fully he meets these first requirements, the more others will join him in his new life.

There will be some persons, of course, who have a need to throw stones—either to compensate for or to forget their own sins. But he accepts this. The *real* people will go forward with him when he is ready.

# CHAPTER 8. WHEN TIME RUNS OUT

Never once in my experience in our spiritual laboratory did I see a person come to the *ultimate moment,* facing the end of earthly life, who did not make a beginning and then come to know in the deepest sense who he or she was. There was not one exception in twenty-three years.

Why should this be?

Once we had a brilliant young man in our church who felt an inner pressure which created a state of nausea before any event during which he came in contact with strangers. He felt competitive with his father and brothers; he was not free to love his wife, except physically. In time he developed cancer of the stomach.

Before and during his illness we spent much time together, and I came to know well his character and attitudes. His analytical mind had to have iron-clad proof for what couldn't be proved but which can be known through faith. He was hypercritical: once a year I gave the Sermon on the Mount from memory in our morning services. He used to sit in the audience, checking on me. If I missed a word, he would look up at me accusingly.

Two hours before he expired, he became free. He was actually radiant. He asked me to give the Sermon on the Mount, saying, "Today I will not check on you." He showed love to his father and brothers and he drew his wife into the oxygen tent, showing his tender affection. At the moment of what I term "graduation," he was transformed; he spoke enthusiastically of the next dimension.

I said to my son, who was his physician, "You must have sedated him heavily, he was so happy."

"I gave him nothing," was the answer.

"How do you account for this?"

"The answer is easy. His problems were solved," said my son.

## WHY MANY CANNOT MAKE A BEGINNING

Dr. William Burkhart was right. With his problems solved, this man became free. As death approaches, the bonds are broken; the prison doors opened; the more disconcerting mental vibrations stilled; the real self freed.

The Bible speaks of this as being saved "as if by fire." How wonderful that it can happen, even though it is so late!

Could there also be another reason why in the ultimate moment persons become free? It seems to me that the fear of death is the mother of all fears. Never have I seen a person, though riddled with anxiety and fear, come up to the end of their time without a sense of peace. All fears and anxiety left. Why? As they came to face the experience they knew as death, they no longer feared it. Overcoming this root fear, all other fears and anxieties were canceled.

## TWO ILLUSTRATIONS

There was a member of my church whom I tried unsuccessfully to reach for seventeen years. His wife and two daughters were deeply devoted to the church and to the life of the spirit. They had a meaningful faith. But he made light of everything that was precious to them. Now and then I had lunch with him and he overwhelmed me with his wisecracks. When his two daughters were married, he was the life of the party, but he jarred people because he dealt lightly and cheaply with things that were sacred and private.

One day his wife called me and said that her husband was in the hospital. She felt that maybe he was ready to see me. I went. The day before he had gone to his doctor for a routine checkup and had been hustled immediately into the hospital. What he had suspected for some time was true. He had a serious heart condition. A few hours after he arrived in the hospital he had a severe attack. I found him in an oxygen tent as I entered his room.

"If you hadn't come, I'd have thought you were slipping," he remarked. He was still in character. "Now don't get the idea I'm scared," he added. "I'm not. You know very well I don't scare easily, but it's become very clear to me that I've been running from God all my life. In fact, I believe that the faster I ran from Him, the closer I got to Him."

I pulled up a chair and continued to listen. I slipped my hand into the oxygen tent and put it on one of his. He did not withdraw, but grasped my hand—squeezed it. He went on talking and what he said was very interesting.

Among other things he went back into his boyhood. His father had been killed in an accident when he was seven years old, and he had grown up without a father. He idealized the minister of his church. He was mischievous in Sunday school. Part of his misbehavior lay in his own insecurity, so he covered it up by taking various roles—by making it difficult for the teacher, by annoying the class—all in an effort to get attention. One day he exhausted his teacher's patience. She went to the minister, who, in his exasperation, grabbed the boy and led him to the door, pushed him out, and said, "When you're ready to behave you can return."

The man looked up at me and said, "Now don't get the idea that I'm critical of that minister. He had every right to do what he did. I'm simply saying that from where I was then, this was a real rejection. I lost my father, and at the funeral the minister said, 'The Lord giveth and the Lord taketh away.' This made me hate God. And then when the minister kicked me out of the church, I was rejected again, for I had loved him, adored him, looked up to him. Well, think of me whatever you will," he continued, "I have not been in a church since except when my two daughters were married. I didn't even go when they were christened."

He kept on in this vein. Finally I said to him, "Be still for a little. Just let us be silent."

"Are you going to pray for me?" he asked.

I said, "Would you like to pray?"

"Let's pray in silence," he replied.

As I held his hand I felt him relax. Peace seemed to come into his body, and in due time I was aware he was asleep. I stayed with him a while and then left.

When I returned later that night, he greeted me with, "Oh, I'm so glad you came! I wanted to talk more." He proceeded to outline a number of things that represented unfinished business in his life. "It's asking a lot of you," he said, "but would you go to see these people and straighten things out for me? I'll give you three signed checks and make whatever restitution is necessary." He told me how much money he had in the bank. I agreed to go.

I went to the people involved and made the restitution. They accepted the money. When the unfinished business was taken care of, I returned to him.

"Do you think I can be forgiven for the way I wronged them?" he asked.

"God forgave you before you ever did it," I assured him. "All you need to do is to forgive others and forgive yourself and forgiveness becomes automatic. You have confessed, you have made restitution, you have repented. Now you're forgiven. Of that you can be sure."

"I would like very much to be baptized," he said then.

"I'll be glad to baptize you," I told him. "What does baptism mean to you?"

He went on to tell me what he felt it would mean to him, and I was moved by his understanding of the sacrament. He said that since he had come out of the Church of the Brethren he would like to be immersed.

"Well, you're in an oxygen tent," I pointed out. "I can only immerse your hands and your feet."

"Also immerse my chin and my mouth," he requested, "because I've said many things I did not mean." I did this.

Then he asked me to anoint his body, because this is part of the practice of the Church of the Brethren. I got some baby oil from one of the nurses and anointed his body.

I took him into the membership of the church and later gave the sacraments to his wife and daughters and their husbands. It was a remarkable family experience.

In the course of our time together, he said two unforgettable things. One was: "I'm not only aware of all I missed, but I'm aware of all I made other people miss." But perhaps the most penetrating thing he said was this: "I'm not only aware of all the wrong I did, but of all the good I never got around to do."

Then he expired.

It was the profound experience of one who in the ultimate moment finally became free of a past that had held him in chains.

In his particular profession he was brilliant and creative; in the city where he lived there are monuments to his genius; but to those of us who were with him in the ultimate moment, there is a different kind of a monument; there is a memory that has wings, brightened with visions of truth that will never leave us.

Another man I ministered to was one who seemed unable to die. It was his physician who originally contacted me.

As I entered his room and walked to his bed, he regarded me with startled eyes and demanded, "Who are you?" When I told him he said quickly, "Pray for me."

"Let us visit a while if you don't mind," I returned.

And so we talked.

It came out that he was under great tension, emotionally bound up, and frightened. Repeatedly he begged me to pray for him. When I said, "Will *you* pray?", he replied, "But I can't pray."

I have always been slow to pray with people for two reasons. It is possible in praying with them to drive their feelings underground. Moreover, then I am not aware of where the person is in his own thinking and feeling. By getting the person himself to pray, I can learn where he is in his thinking and feeling. I also learn the direction he is facing. Moreover, he is becoming active. He is expressing himself. If I pray for him, I'm doing something *to* him. If I get him to pray, I'm doing something *through* him. And so with this man, when I couldn't get him to pray or even to talk, I suggested that we have a silent prayer. This we did.

When I returned later that night, he was wide awake. I pulled up a chair and sat by his bed and said, "Let us be silent together." I thought surely he would begin to talk but he didn't. I stayed with him an hour. When the twelve o'clock hour came, I stood and said, "Is there something you would like to say to me? I have a feeling you want to talk." He simply said again, "Pray for me." At this point I did and left with a promise to see him in the morning.

But just as I was about to enter the elevator, something seemed to say to me, "You better go back." I did. As I walked into his room he said, "Oh, I'm so glad you came back," and with that he began to talk.

It soon became clear why he could not leave this dimension. He was involved in a life in which he did not believe. He had much unfinished business. For a number of years he had spent Saturday afternoon with one woman and Wednesday afternoon and evening with another woman. He provided well for both. They did not know of each other, and his wife was without knowledge of either of them.

He asked me to call his lawyer, and together we three worked out a plan by which he not only could make restitution, but by which his unfinished business could be completed. Then he asked me the familiar question, "Is there any hope for me?"

"You have confessed; you have made restitution," I said. "Now you can be forgiven. In fact, God is ready to forgive you." I supported this by Scripture.

He said, "I have never been baptized, would you baptize me?" And as I completed the sacrament, he asked, "Now could I receive communion?" And I gave him the bread and the cup. Then he asked if he could be taken into the church. And so I gave him the church vows and took him into the membership of the church.

Then he said, "Will you call my wife so I can confess to her?"

His lawyer inserted himself at this point. "Oh, don't do that," he exclaimed. "You've done everything you can to right the wrong. For you to confess to her now and then leave her is a bigger burden than she can bear."

He turned to me and asked, "Must I confess to her?"

I went along with the lawyer's view. "No," I said. "I will do everything I can to minister to her in the future."

He expired quietly, and there was the "peace that passeth understanding" reflected in his face.

His attorney and I carried out the program we had agreed to, that the plan of restitution might be fulfilled. In due time, his wife came into our church and having worked through her grief, she has grown into great freedom and to great stature. While she's still a widow, she's remarkably alive and free. It became clear that she had not been blind to all that was going on but had felt it useless to pry, to threaten, to censure him. She had accepted him as he was and had seen him as he could be, feeling that if she saw him clearly as he could be, one day the requirement would be met for him to become that person.

## HOW ABOUT SUICIDE?

You may ask, "How about people who commit suicide—do they before they expire become free?" It is a good question. Suicide can either have the elements of a tantrum or the final escape.

I have known suicides that were "faked," but went further than the person intended. In a fit of anger, or during frustration, or in a moment of rejection, a person may feel like punishing those whom he believes to be responsible for his pain. "They'll be sorry," he says to himself. Such suicides may even be seriously undertaken. These have the element of the tantrum.

But most suicides are undertaken by persons who cannot face life anymore. The anxiety or depression is too great for them to bear. They feel they must put an end to their suffering.

Others, overanxious about the future, fearing a sickness such as cancer, choose to get out of the way, not only to escape suffering but to save their loved ones the burden of nursing care. Others, caught in a moral crisis or threatened with failure, choose suicide in the belief that the insurance money can save the situation.

If a person succeeds, in our way of thinking, he made a serious mistake. He on his own has terminated his life in the physical body: he has given up his brain. He is now in his energy or thought-body, for when our bodies can no longer serve us, God gives us a *spiritual body*. To initiate this ourselves means that we go into the next dimension with problems unsolved.

And yet, while this is the way it looks to us, we must remember that we did not walk in his shoes. Thus our judgments must be tempered by compassion and understanding.

# CHAPTER 9. WHEN AWARENESS COMES

We come now to the last chapter of Part I, all of which is devoted to describing ways by which a person can make a beginning and grow toward wholeness and the fulfillment of his true destiny.

## WHAT IS AWARENESS?

Awareness is aliveness as a person. Aliveness in terms of his own being and aliveness and alertness to others and to the state of being all about him. One is aware to the degree to which he is responsive to outside stimuli and meanings and to inner reality. One is aware to the degree to which he is sensitive to all states of being; to the degree to which he is free to love and be loved.

How might we illustrate the meaning of awareness? Once I was talking to a group of professional men in the Variety Club of my city. After the talk, we had a good discussion and at the conclusion they said, "If possible, stay. We're having some entertainment. A girl is going to dance for us." I had another engagement, so I declined and left. As I was leaving, the girl who was to dance for them came out for her first number. We stood for a moment face to face. She was scantily clothed. She had blond hair and blue eyes. I went on. On the way down the steps I said to myself, "She looks like our daughter." Further down the steps I said to myself, "She *is* our daughter." This was for me a moment of true awareness.

May I ask you, how many of those men would have let their own daughter dance before them with little or no clothing? The answer is simple, not one. Why then did they let this girl? They were just not aware enough to recognize that they should think of this girl as their daughter.

We could carry it further, how many of us could bear to see a baby crying for food and not feed it? Be naked and not clothe it? Be sick and not cared for? Not one of us. We would give the last thing we had to help. But there are millions of babies in the world who are hungry. Millions are sick; millions are cold. Why is it that we Americans do not go further to alleviate this suffering? Does not the answer lie in the quality of our awareness?

If I am aware, I know how you feel. In time then, you can come to know how you feel. If I know your feelings, and rightly assess where you are, you are fully understood. What can mean more to you?

Some years ago a boy in our city beat a woman sixty-five years of age, giving her a double jaw-fracture. The court asked me to accept custody. I went with him to East Rich Street in our city, an area known as the snake belt, where he lived with his grandmother and two aunts. I never saw more hostile people. The whereabouts of his parents were unknown.

Why did he beat this old woman? He was doing some work for her, and she slapped him. Then he attacked her. Why? Because he was angry at his grandmother.

I secured a new home for him. He at first would not talk to me, except when in the car. I let him steer and then he would talk! It took him two years to learn to respond to love. In due time he graduated from high school and college. He was a captain in the air force during the war. Today he is an outstanding man in our city, but he lives with his family in the east end of the snake belt. One day I asked him, "Why do you live here?"

"Why? I must be the boy a boy should be for five hundred boys." I asked him what he meant. "You were not just you. You were both of us—yourself and me until I could be myself." I was not really as much as he thinks, but insofar as I was, his understanding of this indicated real awareness.

But we need to go further. Awareness is a quality not only

of aliveness but openness. One is only aware insofar as all apartness is canceled. Nothing is hidden that cannot stand the light of day. What is in me that I must keep secret is devastating to me as a person. I become what I must keep secret. Part of me is withheld. I am two people, one behind the curtain of secrecy; the other with people. Thus I am split; I am not whole; and cannot be truly aware. So awareness involves the whole self, open and free, with the whole book open and no pages hidden. Open and whole, I then can respond to and be sensitive to those around me.

Once John Donne expressed a great thought. He said: "No man is an island, entire of itself, every man is a piece of the continent, a part of the main . . . and therefore never send to know for whom the bell tolls, it tolls for thee." That which means the fulfillment of one means the fulfillment of all. That which means the denial of one means, in a deep sense, the denial of all.

## IS AWARENESS THE PRELUDE TO OR THE FRUIT OF GROWTH?

I have come increasingly to the recognition that insight is less a quality in the freeing process than it is a result of it. Awareness is part of insight. I must have insight to become aware; if I am really aware, then I have insight.

When awareness comes, therefore, maybe one has already made a beginning. As awareness comes, the person continues to begin. We never, as we have been saying, arrive. We are always in the process of beginning. Life, as we shall see in Part II, is a series of beginnings. Completions are ever withheld.

Of prime importance is the beginning step. And the initial beginning becomes a chain reaction of beginnings. One keeps on doing his best if in fellowship with one significant person or with a creative group. The farther he goes, the greater will be his awareness. The more aware he is, the more he will keep making beginnings. So does it not seem that awareness is a by-product of growth as well as a stimulus of ongoing beginnings?

As I look at my life, my real beginnings came through the influence of persons and in my relationship with others who were trying to make beginnings. This included a period of psychoanalytic treatment which helped, but which left me with many blind spots. Finally I was led to commit myself to a life of prayer. I was dissatisfied with myself. I was determined to learn prayer-power. I organized groups in prayer research. I continued to make beginnings. But even prayer and these groups for a time were a substitute for really facing up to some of my real needs. I was very busy and this was in a sense an escape for me. I held too tight to the reins of leadership. I put pressure on my staff in subtle ways.

Awareness came to me slowly. In fact, since I am no longer the leader of our spiritual laboratory, I see more clearly where I was and where I could have been. When I really became aware, then growth became manifest where before overactivity was due to the fact that I stopped making beginnings.

Here I want only to sketch its meaning in my own life. As my awareness grew, I not only came to understand myself, but I could understand how another person felt and could then act from the vantage point of where he was rather than where I was. I then did not need to overreact to temper, to depressed states, to criticism.

For some time I could be aware of persons far removed from me physically while insensitive to those at hand. I could give many illustrations. I was vividly and personally aware of the hungry children of the world. I could sense the desolation of persons with whom I was working as a minister or counselor; yet I created barriers between myself and some of my staff members and in strange ways put pressures on my children—even rejected them. I could see so clearly the needs and shortcomings of others —the need to be adored, the inability to think of anyone but oneself, the drive to seek praise or shame—but I could not see many of my own needs and shortcomings, or if I did, I could do nothing about them. I could see others use persons for worthwhile undertakings, then drop them and go on to enlist someone else, leaving the individuals with a feeling of rejection. In my busyness, I did the very same thing without knowing it.

What I am saying is that real awareness came slowly to me. Much came only to a marked degree in the last fifteen years of my work in our laboratory, but even more has come as I have observed others walk in paths where I once trod.

What we are therefore saying is that awareness accompanies and nourishes personal growth. As awareness deepens, growth expands; it has more purpose; the search becomes increasingly more personal and yet releases more potential to help others. What we often call insight may be an enemy of true awareness; so-called "insights" can be conversation pieces, ideas we throw at people rather than actually making a real beginning and moving toward solutions. When we really make beginnings, then we increasingly know ourselves and understand others in our presence. The more we grow, the greater our awareness becomes, until it can not only include the suffering mass of mankind, but even those in the next dimension.

In a meeting with George Washington Carver, in an early morning meditation at a student volunteer convention, something happened to me I shall never forget. I was moved by the experience, though then it did not serve as a beginning for me but instead an experience to share with others.

At the close of the meeting, I said, "Dr. Carver, you have traveled a long, hard path. But instead of being bitter, you are loving. How do you account for it?"

He gazed at me for a time and then said, "No man is big enough to hate; every man is big enough to love." He paused briefly and then continued in some such way as this: "Now love was once a concept to which I subscribed, but which I didn't feel. I talked it when really I didn't feel it. I acted it when within I felt rage, but it was too dangerous for me to express my real feelings. But as I came to look at the peanut, at the sweet potato, at the wonderful world about me, I began to sense God in the simplest things, in all living things, in His wonderful world, in every man and in myself. Then love was no longer an idea; it was the state of my whole being. Love dictated the quality of my awareness."

"Then this awareness came as a result of meeting some other conditions?" I asked.

"Yes, it is the reward of growth, understanding, endless seeking."

"Then it is not only a reward but a guarantee that the search never comes to an end?"

"Yes."

I have often quoted these words of Dr. Carver for they have stayed with me ever since. Dr. Carver was aware.

Mrs. Rackam Holt, who wrote a great biography of Dr. Carver, told me that she walked with him in the early morning and that often he would take several hours to move a very short distance. "He was totally alive to all living things and totally attentive to all persons," she said to me.

## CONCLUSION

As we travel the five roads of man's spiritual destiny, we will see the meaning of awareness along all the roads. We will then see more clearly what Dr. Carver said to me a long time ago, that awareness is the fruit of growth and the stimulus to further growth.

# PART II.   THE UNFAILING RESOURCES

## CHAPTER 10.   IN MAN, LIFE IS SEEKING ULTI- MATE FULFILLMENT

By looking at a large variety of human situations we have seen how persons can make a beginning. We have discovered some of the guiding principles and seen how these relate to man's struggle to move out of bondage into freedom.

Now as we turn to examine the unfailing resources available to him, we discover the encouraging fact that life is seeking fulfillment in man.

In Genesis we read, "Then the Lord God formed man of dust from the ground, and breathed into his nostrils the breath of life; and man became a living being" (Gen. 2:7). What a wonderful statement about the great moment when man arrived at a sense of his being. This was the supreme moment. For if one day with the Lord is as a thousand years, this moment may well have reached across millennia.

### THE NATURE OF LIFE

Life is dynamic; it breaks over every vessel made to contain it. We cannot put new wine in old bottles, for they will break. Life seeks its fulfillment in the single cell, in the person, and in the total fellowship. Only when the best interests of all are in focus is life fulfilled.

Life has evolved from a single cell to its amazing fulfillment in man with his unlimited possibilities. We observe progress and we therefore assume purpose. How many eons have elapsed since the fireball became the planet, the crystal the cell, the jelly-fish the saurian, and the time when man first felt aspirations which were to lay the foundations of a way of life, we do not know.

Gerald Heard says, "As a man has by his striving become con-scious, as he becomes aware of his inborn need to experience, to learn, to understand, he must, if he is to be true to his inner need to fulfill his true nature, grasp the reasons why it is in his nature to strive, to seek, to find; how his condition has aligned him for his destiny, what forces have energized him for this effort, what goals his trained powers could attain. For man is the one creature that is not driven by inbuilt forces that impel him to develop an inborn racial competence. He is drawn by a dream of a future of yet undisclosed excellence. He does not fulfill himself by precedent alone but surpasses himself by prescience." [1]

## IS THERE A LAG IN MAN'S GROWTH?

Man is always striving. He never gives up. Ever he is seeking to solve his problems. As we have seen, it is man's nature to grow, and it is God's infinite grace that provides the possibility for man's search to be rewarded. It is true that in the chronicle of man's pilgrimage, crowns and thrones have perished, king-doms have risen and waned, strange phenomena have appeared, moral growth has alternated with moral decay, trial and error have gone on. But now, irreplaceable man feels a new urgency because of two perils that confront him: the threat of a system that seeks to coerce life and to conscript the soul, and the threat of nuclear suicide.

Though I feel there is a lag in man's growth, I am not un-mindful of the countless persons all over the world, in humble or more exalted paths, who are great beacon lights to those who are striving toward solutions in every area of human research, the purpose of which is to provide all that is necessary for the health of the body and the achievement of the wholeness of the individual.

Nevertheless, there is evidence of a lag among the peoples of the free world, and especially among those who adhere to the way of Jesus. This most dynamic and exciting way of life has brought man to the gateway of the Golden Age, so that he has within his grasp the resources to solve all the problems plaguing his world. Man can learn to know who he is and communicate his wholeness and integrity until peace grows in the home, the market place, and in the complex relations of peoples and nations.

What are the forces responsible for the lag in man's growth?

1. *Might not our materialism be a root cause of our growth lag?* We will discuss the unfailing resource in all that is given, especially the resources for our nourishment and nurture. We will see the problem that takes place when men get their goals confused, neglecting their own growth and the enrichment of their own life. We will see that beneath most of the world's injustices, its selfishness and narcissism, its clashing ambitions, are the desires of human souls directed toward wrong goals. These fundamental yearnings of the human soul, these persistent hungers, are disastrous and destructive unless directed by spiritual values toward spiritual goals.

Buddha saw desire as the very core of life and also the heart of the world's trouble. He said in effect: "You must free your heart of all desire, denude your heart of every want, and in utterly passionless existence you shall find rest." Jesus saw that yearning was the motive force of life. He would not destroy but exalt it. His message was that men should seek first the kingdom of God and its righteousness and all other things would be added.

Today is it not the goal of millions to get and to keep things, while ignoring the need to become whole persons? If this is true, perhaps this is one reason for the lag. Some years ago Bruce

Hutchinson of Winnipeg said, "If America becomes great with her comfort, she will be the first people who ever did in the history of the world."

2. *Might not another reason for the lag be that millions never become persons because they get lost in the mass?* Are they not so much a part of the herd that they have lost their peculiar sense of uniqueness, their feeling of identity?

In the Introduction and later on in our discussion we have seen the danger of the person becoming a part of the collective huddle, where he is desolate and lonely.

The Russian philosopher Berdyaev says, "In the very act of affirming himself, man has lost himself. He has conquered the earth; he has created the marvels, but his assurance in himself has gone. Dwarfed and insignificant, he is left to contemplate the vast space he has discovered. When man broke away from the spiritual moorings of his life, he tore himself from the deep and went to the shallows."

Does this not mean that as a person he has no meaning, or that his only meaning derives from being part of the crowd? This is a relationship in which the person has no real identity. If he comes to the group totally on its terms, then membership is a denial of his own individuality. He does not think, he paraphrases; he has no convictions, he chants the group thoughts; he is a slave, for he submits to the group stereotypes.

This relationship in which the person loses his sense of being, this situation in which originality is gone, is a training ground for dictatorship. A perceptive social scientist pointed out that Hitler did not usurp power, but had it thrust upon him. It is almost frightening to see lost persons make their condition more desperate by asking to be pushed around and mastered—to have someone else think for them.

Out of this grows a dwarfing dependency, resulting in the fact that millions seek security, not opportunity, and have lost the capacity to take a risk.

Does this not account for the growth of communism in the last forty-three years? Today it controls one-third of the human race, and as Charles Malik says, "It has softened up to a degree the other two-thirds." Is its growth inevitable? If one says "yes," then he has substantiated Marxist propaganda.

3. *Might a third reason for the lag be the fact that many people operate on the assumption that life is an accident, that man is a cosmic accident, and therefore love is nothing more than a spasm of the nerves?* If the universe is the result of an accidental and a meaningless explosion of energy, if the mind is the supreme result of this accident, then we have not only a basis for the lag, but the reason for moral paralysis and the far-reaching degree of anxiety and stress.

What is our answer to this faith based on a negative assumption? Perhaps there are no complete answers, but there are reasons that reason knows and reasons that faith suggests.

Is not the very existence and persistence of the urge to believe, despite all that has been done to kill it, the best evidence that faith is reality that passes knowledge?

Joan of Arc is sure she hears voices, but she is burned at the stake without witnessing the fulfillment of her highest hopes. Savonarola consecrates himself to the moral redemption of Florence, and his enemies kill him in the name of the God he loves and serves in faith; he does not see the fruition of his hopes.

Tyndale gives the people of England the Bible in their own tongue, but he is hounded like a common felon until his body is brutally dishonored and his ashes thrown to the winds; John Bunyan spends thirteen years in the Bedford jail because he gives testimony to his soul's knowledge of God, but he goes into the next dimension not knowing he has lifted the world to a simpler and more sublime idea of the eternal. Each of these endured, and millions like them, nameless and unknown, as if they had a glimpse of the invisible.

By an imperial act of faith we must assume that life is meaningful if we are to find meaning there. If we just drift along with the eye alert to catch some sign of significance, we will not find it. And if we go through life responding only to outer stimuli, we will not find it. Life will be an idle tale.

But if we say, "I believe there is meaning and purpose in life, something noble and beautiful and exacting at the heart of life," and if we begin to respond to that purpose, then we shall find it.

There is no other way. As we must plant the acorn to find the universal forces that produce the oak, so we, by faith, must put moral purpose and passion into life to find fellowship with the Person at the heart of life. In a beautiful parable, Gilbert Frensen says, "I sowed my enemy's field with corn that God might continue to exist." That is deep insight. He did not create God by his act of forgiving love, but he found the reality of God for his own soul by so doing. He put meaning into life and found meaning there. Faith is not a thing one loses; it is something by which one continues to shape his life.

Our first answer to the charge that life is accidental is that man believes he is created, that there is a Person or something personal at the heart of life. This faith persists, so it must have its secret answer.

There is a second answer. Life has developed from simpler forms to a supreme material reality that is the human body, and to the greater reality, the mind which says "I." This development indicates a plan; a plan indicates purpose; purpose indicates mind.

There is a third answer. Once I had a short interview with Albert Einstein. I asked the great man to indicate the mathematical chance that the universe was an accident, that mind was accidental. Dr. Einstein wrote a fraction I could not read. After a moment's thought he turned to me and said, "How often would you have to put a tea kettle on the stove for it to freeze?" I said to him, "Dr. Einstein, I can't answer that." He then went on to say, "If you do it often enough it will freeze, for there is a mathematical chance that it will happen."

As I pondered it, I thought, how many times would one have to throw up type before it composed the Sermon on the Mount? I have talked with a number of great persons of profound intellectual capacity who point out that today the laws of chance are a science, that they know the age of the earth and, to some extent, when life began. They also know that in the beginning the protein molecule had to exist. This theory is profoundly complex, but these men point out that we can no longer say that the protein molecule was built up by the random churning of chemicals. By the laws of chance, this could not have occurred accidentally in the time available.

Roland B. Gittelsohn quotes William S. Beck, physician and bio-chemist: "When one reflects on the stupendous complexity of the living organism, it is entirely reasonable to doubt that it could have arisen as the result of a chance event completely physical in character."[2]

The more we look at life and man, the more it is plain that he is not only a higher degree of life than any other, but that in him is revealed a different quality of life. Edmund W. Sinnot had this to say on this point: "Man . . . is so different from the beasts that he is another sort of being. Although he has clambered up the evolutionary stairway, he has in the process passed a critical point where he became not simply the highest form of life but a different creature from any of those that had preceded him."[3]

With this George Gaylord Simpson agrees; as he looks comparatively at man and all previous forms of life, he says, "An absolute difference in kind and not only a relative difference of degree." He goes on to say, "It is still false to conclude that man is *nothing but* the highest animal or the most progressive product of organic evolution. He is also a fundamentally new sort of animal and one in which, although organic evolution continues on its way, a fundamentally new sort of evolution has also appeared."[4]

Many of the great scientific minds as they look at the universe feel that there is not only evidence of administration but that it is friendly to man. The late Arthur H. Compton, Nobel Prize winner in physics, said, "The chance that a world such as ours should occur without intelligent design becomes more and more remote as we learn of its wonders."[5]

George Russell Harrison, Dean of the School of Science at the Massachusetts Institute of Technology, writes: "It is not difficult for a scientist to see the hand of God in the patterns which protons, neutrons, and electrons take in forming atoms, and those which the atoms take to form molecules, molecules to form cells, cells to form tissues, organs, and bodies, and bodies to form social aggregates. . . . The basic tenets of all great religions, the distilled spiritual wisdom of humanity, coincides closely with what science reveals in nature. The universe is based on order, not on chaos and chance."[6]

These, then, may be reasons for the lag in man's growth. Today over the whole world there is a psychological, perhaps, more accurately, a philosophical or ideological revolution. There seems to be a growing awareness that man cannot continue to evade coming to know who he is. I believe the stimulus is available to awaken persons to overcome the lag and respond to truth that will never let man go.

## WHAT IS THE BASIS OF HOPE?

Concerning man, there are three profound bases of hope: First, man is more than an animal; he has a destiny beyond the power of words to describe or the universal language of music to portray.

If man were descended from the apes, the apes would be more civilized than man. The fossil skull of a chimpanzee living millions of years ago shows a much greater brain case than any contemporary chimpanzee. Chimpanzees would therefore seem to be in the process of devolution, rather than evolution.

Man has become more developed than any other animal. The gorilla, as an illustration, has made a kind of foot out of his hand. The free movement of man's thumb over his hand may seem inconsequential but in it lies, to a great degree, the secret of man's tremendous power. It was Kagawa, the great Japanese leader, who caught the spirit of it when he said:

I cannot invent
New things,
Like the airships,
Which sail
On silver wings;
But today
A wonderful thought
In the dawn was given,
And the stripes on my robe,
Shining from wear,
Were suddenly fair,
Bright with a light
Falling from Heaven—
Gold, and silver, and bronze
Lights from the windows of Heaven.
And the thought
Was this:
That a secret plan
Is hid in my hand;
That my hand is big,
Big,
Because of this plan.
That God, Who dwells in my hand,
Knows this secret plan
Of the things He will do for the world
Using my hand!

Man is unique in that he remains so long a child. Even in his adulthood, there is the influence of the child in his past. The learning span of a rat is six weeks; the learning span of man is at least twelve years, but the potential span is forever. Maybe this is why Jesus suggested that in order to enter the Kingdom of Heaven, where all is wholeness, we must become as a little child.

The second reason for hope is that man is the ultimate fulfillment of an eternal purpose. As man tunneled up from the dark and the damp, he heard the tools of a Master Workman above him. The longer he struggled, the greater his understanding became and the greater the union he knew with the God in every other man.

Third, at the moment of conception, man is given being and infinite possibilities of development. The resources are here and the understanding can be found for him to achieve wholeness. He has unlimited growth potential. If the life process is to be fulfilled in man, he must come to know and understand who he is until he understands all persons around him. He must know the person he can love until he loves all persons and they are free to love in return.

If man perceives his situation, position and endowment, then he must, with passionate and earnest research, learn how he can cooperate with the life force guiding him. Only then can he become a whole person, communicate his wholeness with others, and finally come to a profound sense of union with God to whose eternal and neverending leadership he responds. In this way he achieves this consummation—becoming a whole person and helping create a relationship in which others may find it.

## MAN IS UNFINISHED

Life is seeking its ultimate fulfillment in man. There is no limit to what he can be and become. Jesus said, "Be ye perfect, even as your father in Heaven is perfect." What was he saying? Man shall become whole and join in creating a relationship in which others become whole.

Man has come a long way, but he is unfinished. The challenge now is for his wisdom to match his power, for his spiritual insight to match his physics. To chart the process of growth, we move on to investigate the most important research waiting to be undertaken seriously.

In the next chapter we will come to a sense of the nameless longings that stir in the heart of every living soul.

# CHAPTER 11. VISIONS OF TRUTH THAT NEVER LET YOU GO

We have said that life seeks to fulfill itself in man. The explosive force of life is in every cell and is manifested in all states of being. When man is real, when he is free at all, he responds. Indeed, when he is no longer disquieted, when he no longer feels the restlessness of one far from the goal that lures him, he has ceased to be human and crept back to the lowlands from which he came. Might we not say that the lost soul is one who feels the pang of no great desire and feels the pain of no lofty discontent? The lost soul is caught in a terrible despond from which he is freed only with great difficulty.

## THE GOTHIC QUALITY OF LIFE

Once in Tulsa, Oklahoma, I was stirred by a church tower that haunted me. I understood why I felt as I did when the story was finally told of a woman who gave a hundred thousand dollars to build this tower but made one stipulation: "That to all succeeding generations it would seem incomplete." The thought prompted me to do some research into the Gothic. It has a special quality; its structure contains stress and strain; its rhythm is that of a bird in flight; its poise is that of a lark seeking its nest at eventide. The Gothic cathedral is never finished; there is always something for the centuries to add. In every groin and spire is the agony of aspiration, the outreach for the unfulfilled and unpossessed.

So, in any observation of those seeking to be the persons that fulfill their real destiny, one becomes aware of souls with nameless longings, hearts with great contradictions and conflicts, human spirits beating against the gates of life and crying,

"Open, open unto me." Such a soul shares with those who know doubts and temptations, conflicts and disquietudes, struggles and aspirations, but above it all, some tyrant dream of truth that will not let him go.

These are Gothic souls, sometimes weary and world-broken, sometimes illumined by the glint of a dawn of which millions have dreamed. We know these souls to be climbing, falling, limping, despairing, rising to climb again, and going onward. If one looks across the pages of history, he sees a great procession, and leading them is One about whom is the shadow of the cross. They are never fully defeated, never fully victorious, but pressing on. "As the hart panteth after the water brook, so panteth my soul after thee, O God."

## LIFE IS A JOURNEY

The above is true for the person unless he is hopelessly caught in the lag of which we have spoken. The freed person reaches forward to that which is ahead, but never arrives at a point when he can say. "Oh, this is the land of my desire; here let me always dwell." Something calls, and the real soul follows, not as a victim but as one fulfilling his destiny. At the core of life is not satisfaction but desire, not a quiet home but a restless road. We shall never understand ourselves or others unless we realize that interwoven into the fabric of every human spirit there is a nameless longing.

A poet once interpreted man by drawing a ladder, the top of which was lost among the clouds; upon it stood a being with outstretched arms and yearning face, crying, "I want! I want!" All of our material civilization is built upon fostering the spirit of want and then in seeking to supply the demands; all education and science recognizes man's outreaching soul and attempts to direct his struggle to fulfill his hunger and satisfy his thirst. Religion is pillared by the infinite longings of the human spirit.

In all areas of the search it is important for man to realize that he finds truth not only by observation but in communion, not only by scientific inquiry but by surrender, not only in the laboratory but in the sanctuary.

Man can denude his soul of dreams; he can free himself of all disturbing aspirations and know what he calls "peace." But it is not "peace"; it is the quietude of death. Real peace is always mingled with the pain of longing. One can come to know peace, but almost at once he feels the pain of conflict. The goal of life is to attain the proper rhythm of peace and pain. People in America have too much "peace"; people in the under-developed areas of the world have too much "pain." Too much peace can mean "death"; too much pain can mean "sickness." The person becoming whole is on the march; he has healthy proportions of peace and pain.

Now the truth is that the higher one's scale of living, the more exquisite is the pain of desire. It is a strange paradox that those who achieve the finest satisfactions know the most passionate hungers.

Jesus knew fundamental human yearnings, for He was always looking forward. He said, "I go to the Father"; always He pointed to a world seeking to be a reality, for He said, "Behold, I make all things new."

We can only understand man if we realize that he is a bundle of desires; his soul is characterized by its outreachings. This pursuit is so basic to life that sensitive people do not know which is the greater gift—finding truth or the privilege of searching for it.

A sculptor, receiving great praise for what was deemed his masterpiece, was seen by friends to be quietly weeping. Asked what brought sorrow on his day of triumph, he said, "But you see, I am satisfied. I feel no torment of difference between what I have done and what I wanted to do. Therefore, I know that my powers have begun to decay."

We have said that the higher one goes, the greater is his longing; the deepest satisfactions beget the deepest longings. The tenderest human love and all its kindly comradeship is a haven of rest for the ships of desire, but it is also a harbor from which to set sail for the calling deeps. Our human loves, indeed, all of our satisfactions, give us a sense of joy and peace. We know that the truest love is the merging of the infinite longing of two human souls. It is not simply the cure of loneliness; it is comradeship in loneliness.

In one of his lyrics, George Herbert says that when God made man He poured into him all the blessings he could contain—love, strength, beauty, wisdom, honor, and pleasure. Just one he withheld. That was rest, the blessing of peace.

## THE JOURNEY SEEMS TO POINT BEYOND THIS DIMENSION

The pagans spoke of "Mother Earth," but if she is our only destiny, if the journey ends in this dimension, then the red dawn would touch men as does the kindling of a hearthfire, the mountains would seem like the massive walls of a garden, and the stars would utter in their own grand way the message that twinkles in the lamplight of a cottage window. But is this really so? Would it not be more accurate to say that man is homeless in the dawn? That the mountain provides not shelter but haunting aspiration? Who can stand under the stars and for a moment feel their peace without, at the same moment, feeling longings that are nameless?

Across the years I have been with great souls in the high moments and in the low; I have been with many in the ultimate moment, and more and more it has become clear that life in this dimension is not a destination but a journey; not an ending but a beginning. This does not mean that I undervalue life in this dimension. I cherish it, but I'm aware that in this dimension there are so many beginnings without final fulfillments—all life's completions seem withheld. What lover ever felt he came to the end of love? What poet, what musician, what prophet, what searcher, what saint felt he had come to the end? None! Always they glimpse visions of truth that never let them go.

If life is not destined for such heights, then the best of it is mockery. We are here to make ships that shall never sail the sea, to lay foundations upon which shall rise no cathedral groin and agonizing spire, to love and see our love turn to dust. In such an existence, deepest longings are but the laughter of a careless universe.

No, there is another view. Life is not a mockery, for at its core is a truth for which the soul of man craves. Life is given meaning by the soul's loyalty to its goal, its underlying faithfulness to its true destiny.

## THERE IS A THREE-FOLD STRUGGLE

Life is a difficult journey, involving great struggle. This struggle is experienced in three realities.

*The first aspect of the struggle is the individual's struggle with himself.* This may be the toughest battle. Who was it who said, "He that rules his own spirit is greater than he who takes a city" (Prov. 16:32)?

However good and evil came into the world, they are strangely mixed in the nature of man. We see this in the slothful content which makes for comfortable dwelling in the swampy lowlands. It is observable not only in those who do wrong, but in those who refuse to do the good that they have an opportunity to do. On the other hand, we see a winged desire that would build a cathedral in the verdant hills, as seen in those who are true to the highest good, though tempted by the evil. The earth cries, "You belong to me," and Heaven whispers, "Your home is here." Instinct says, "Your way to happiness is through your animal nature"; aspiration cries, "O soul, you were meant for climbing."

The nature and intensity of the struggle to become whole, and its success or failure, will depend only to a small degree on what the person inherits from the past experience of the race, though in Part I we pointed out that this is a factor. But, as we made clear in Chapter 2, basically the outcome of the struggle depends on all that has happened to the person and through him since the moment of conception. It depends on whether the person is free to live, using his gifts from the past, or whether he is in bondage to the past. If a person is free to love, then he can be a person without the need to depreciate himself, without excessive need for support or praise. He is, in other words, the person who is becoming whole.

He will now either be able to deal with temptation or surrender to it. A soul cannot be evil, and a person who is true to the highest longings of his spirit is not evil. He is a victim of his nature only when he refuses or is not free to respond to the Divine Spirit. The God-image, the whole person, what he might be, is calling to the self he is.

There is no need to describe the actual struggle that goes on in every life. The person next to you is bearing a heavy burden. There are doubts to transform into great faith; there are hungers to exalt; there are disappointments to overcome and patience to win, truth to be known, insight to find and enshrine in behavior, freedom to be and to win.

Each person must struggle to grow from the distortion of himself into the likeness of the God-image. The signs of this image are a life marked by giving not getting, caring not ignoring, and responsible action. Each person must learn to get only in order to dedicate, rather than to keep. Beyond this, the God-image is evidenced in a person becoming whole.

In each person there is strife between comfortable illusion and the disturbing truth. The struggle goes on. The harvest is either the bulwark of a finer civilization in great social terms, or the melancholy ruins of a society crumbling to dust. The harvest is in a person who moves toward excellence in those relationships—in friendship, in family life, and in other relations—that lead to maximum fulfillment.

*A second aspect of the struggle is with the environment.* In the person's relationship with other people, the struggle within often becomes intensified because he knows something of the psychology of contrast. Here, because he isn't able to compete, he experiences defeated ambitions, blasted hopes, unrequited loves, lonely separations, the rearing and charging of his sensitive soul against the injustices and cruelties and concerns of the world.

Many of these are more serious when, as we have been saying, the person hasn't come to a sense of his own being.

The question is not, shall a man deal with frustration, but how shall he deal with it. The cross is an eternal witness of what God can do with frustration. There is so much of life that denies faith in a good God, so much that seems the ruthless march of a vast indifference, that faith will need again and again to call upon all its reserves to save the day from despair.

Now and then we meet one who says something like this: "I have traveled the world; I have risen to the suns; I have passed athwart the great waste places of the sky; I have discovered the place where the very shadow of Being dries out and ends; I have gazed into the gulf and cried, 'Father, where art Thou?' But no answer came save the sound of the eternal storm that rages uncontrolled. We are orphans, you and I."

But there is another interpretation, and it is by men who have known life to be fully as difficult and bewildering as anyone who would say the foregoing. In the very consecration of their sufferings they have found strength and confidence. Defeat and loss have become a stairway sloping in the darkness up to God. It is not the circumstances of life that break or uplift us; it is the interpretation we put upon the circumstances. This is a matter of the soul. The soul that fights for the imperial right to believe will find the data for belief even in life's darkest valley. For the soul can make the circumstances of life serve it. The soul can bring its own climate to life and live in its own environment.

Actually, it seems that growth often takes place most fully in the midst of struggle. I have seen a person suffer from a nervous breakdown and come out of it and move toward wholeness. I have observed other persons grow from birth into freedom and great fulfillment. But in either case can we not say that most of the treasures of life are found in the dark? Out of the great defeats men weave the fabric of great victories, if they keep in mind who they are and to Whom they belong. We pointed this out as one of the principles in Chapter 1. Few hearts are noble that have not been broken. It is not security that develops the human spirit, but danger and accepted opportunity. If prosperity means only houses, automobiles, refrigerators, mighty bombs and bombers—all important in their place, but with no life that transcends them—then we are lost.

Nothing can ever happen to beat us so long as we are not deceived by false optimism or blinded by easy and futile philosophy, but maintain souls true to Him to Whom we belong.

> The bravest battle that ever was fought
> Should I tell you where and when?
> On the maps of the world you'll find it not,
> 'Twas fought in the souls of men.[1]

A soul must contend with the wickedness and wrongs of the world. No one who knows the love and peace of a happy home life can be content unless he gives his best to help others find it. No one can have a sense of security without giving his life to make it available to others. No one with peace in his heart can be satisfied unless he does his utmost to aid in the building of a peaceful community, nation, and world. He cannot be satisfied to see men so intrigued with the face of death that they have lost sight of the face of Him who is the Prince of Peace. No one can have a basic belief in honesty and refuse to do everything in his power to help people discover those principles of living which make honesty possible within and without their lives.

Ever insurgent let me be,
Make me more daring than devout;
From sleek contentment keep me free,
And fill me with a buoyant doubt.

From compromise and things half-done,
Keep me, with stern and stubborn pride;
And when, at last the fight is won,
God, keep me still unsatisfied.[2]

*A third aspect of the struggle is a higher conflict.* It is the struggle with a God who never lets us go. Ever it is His grace to become known in us.

The brook Jabbok where Jacob wrestled is not simply a Palestinian stream. It runs through every human heart, for no one ever escapes the yearning of God. We see God in the remorse that stabs us awake, the strange, impossible ideal that beckons and lures, the glory of faithful love, the persistent desire that leads one to become whole and help create a relationship in which others become whole. God is always in the middle of our lives.

This is what Francis Thompson was saying in "The Hound of Heaven." God is the source of all longing and the power of all becoming. He is the motive, the power, the direction, the life and the fellowship of the journey.

Let us look for a moment at His nature. What is God like? If He is the impetus and goal of the search, the source of the lure and the longing—if all the pain of longing is our response to God's revelation—then what can we say of His nature?

We might first ask why He is secretive. He lets us see His ways and His works only imperfectly. Clouds and darkness are around Him. His light glimmers through a broken crevice. He leaves a footprint on the road by which to track Him. There are those who feel they can interpret all the ways of the Eternal and define Him with precision. This is not because they know God so well, but because they know Him so little. We trust rather the teacher who, standing in the presence of God, will say,

"I do not know. His ways are past finding out. But this I know
—I love Him and He loves me."

But how often we wish we did know life's mystery. How often
we look toward the unanswering Heavens and cry, "Light, oh
for light!" If only God would reveal Himself, if only He would
make His purposes known that we might understand Him better and love Him more. Why does God plead with men to
serve Him and trust Him, and yet leave them to doubt His
goodness and even His existence? The answer to these questions
is found in the Book of Proverbs: "It is the glory of God to
conceal things" (Prov. 25:2). It is not a reflection upon God
that the disclosure of His high purposes is not more complete;
it is part of His moral splendor. The secretiveness of God is
an element in His Fatherhood. It is not the impotence of God,
but the glory of God, that withholds the fullness of His revelation.

There is the lure of a secret. There is a strange relationship
between the stimulus and the response that lies behind all the
searchings of science and philosophy and religion. Some poten-
tiality is hidden in nature and in life, and in the soul of man
there is a corresponding spirit of insatiable quest. A mighty
telescope now is available in order that the heavens might be
searched for their hidden mysteries, but this is man's answer
to the concealments of God. Like a magnet, an uncharted land
draws a Columbus to America, a Livingstone into the jungle,
and a Captain Scott and Commodore Perry to the lonely and
perilous wastes of the earth's poles. Before the morning stars
sang together, God made the laws that govern the universe,
from the mighty march of the sun to the unfolding of the
daffodil. But He ordained that man discover these laws. God
puts marble in the hills, but He builds no cathedrals. He buries
coal in the earth, but He does not light the fire on the hearth-
stone, nor turn the wheels of industry's mighty engines.

This conviction that we may yet build a better world, that
life can be kinder and more humane, that society may be organized on the basis of altruism rather than selfishness—why does it

persist? Why do the choicest spirits of the race live and give their bodies, a great living sacrifice, for that vision? Why do they not share the despairing fatalism that says, "Life always has been cruel and selfish and it always will be"? Why not postpone all moral victory to some other kind of world where God shall set up His throne and command the kindness of men? Why not? Because God has concealed in the heart of man a divine restlessness, and in the heart of humanity a divine possibility. Somewhere behind the hills awaits the beautiful discovery.

The lure of the secret, the fascination of the unknown—what a blessing to us! There is the patience that waits for capacity. It is because of human limitation that divine revelation is withheld.

And, as we have already pointed out, there is another reason. If God were too obvious, He would become coercive. He gives us enough reason to believe in Him, but not so much that we have to.

As we carry further our adventure, four qualities of God's nature will, I believe, become clear. God is totally present. We cannot ask God to do anything He is not at every moment engaged in. He is active in all of creation and He works in us and through us, though we have power to block Him. So it is always important to realize that, given God's infinite care and our full response, we can realize miracles; the impossible becomes possible. God has ordered the physical world with predictable precision, but He says to us, "You can finish the story any way you like."

We can respond to these visions that call, these longings that will not let us go, or we can refuse. In fact, we can refuse until we are no longer able to feel their lure. The future belongs to us. Each person is free to do with it what he wishes.

So often religious faith and theology are just so many words. Once there were those who knew whole-making experiences and described them. It is so easy for those who come after to end up only with the words.

The hope is that the experience will grow, the research will lead to reality, and finally we not only will be able to put it into words that have meaning to others, but make it a part of our own everyday lives.

As we discuss the qualities of God which make possible the adventures that these pages describe, it must be remembered that many people are influenced by other theological points of view than mine. There is extreme conservatism, for example, elements of which have been, I think, the cause of many unhealthy attitudes. Another viewpoint is so liberal that it substitutes psychology and sociology for theology. Some have been influenced either by neo-orthodoxy or by the thinking of Paul Tillich and Rudolf Bultmann. So there are many points of view, all of which are important for us to understand.

As we go forward together, let it be hoped that there will grow up a theology of human relations, a theology that is understandable, that can be lived in every relationship of life, that is psychologically and sociologically sensitive but, at the same time, has within it a warm and dynamic nature that brings together the fragments of all thinking and learning into the wholeness of a way of life.

# CHAPTER 12.   THE GIVEN IN LIFE

Life, seeking to be fulfilled in man, is an unfailing resource. Nameless longings that ever lure men onward, some tyrant dream of truth that never lets them go, the throb of insatiate desire—these are unfailing resources. They are basic to our living. They are the reason why we look up, why we feel the lure of what is to be, why we are never satisfied, why we ever respond to the restless road.

For eight years it was my privilege to work with one of the greatest souls I have ever known. Once, in an hour when those he sought to lead were unable to see what was so clear to him, his winged spirit said these words:

> It is easy to foot the trodden path,
> Where thousands walked before,
> It is simple to push my fragile bark
> Past reefs of a charted shore.
> I find it good to ride the road
> Where others laid the trail.
> It is well to test the ocean's strength,
> Where others also sailed
> But when a dream enslaves a man,
> A dream of the vast untrod,
> A dream that says, strike out with me,
> Strike out or part with God;
> A dream that leads to an untried path,
> Where unknown tempests blow,
> And the only chart a man can boast
> Is his will that bids him go;
> Ah, then, my soul, bethink yourself,
> For God has spread His scroll
> To test the stuff of your rough-hewn faith
> And the fibre of your soul.[1]

## THE GIFT OF LIFE

At conception we were given life and the gift of being, with infinite possibilities of becoming. Life is a supreme miracle of our existence. We have life; we are life. The bodies we live in have life; we who live in them have life.

The life in our bodies is a mystery. What is it? Where is it? We cannot fully describe it. We know it is in every cell of the body, but we do not know its source save that it comes from God. God is life. No one knows where life is; whether life is in the cell or outside of the cell.

We know aspects of the body's life. One is growth, another movement. The body takes food and builds muscle, bone, and blood. It maintains a balance of acid and alkaline. It maintains the same temperature irrespective of its environment. The body is responsive to a law of growth, for it grew from a single cell into a great brotherhood of cells. When two bodies, one male and one female, come together they can create a new body, a new life.

The body renews itself. When awake it does this by breathing and through the intake of water and food. It achieves amazing renewal when it sleeps. Old cells lose themselves in new ones, so that each body becomes new over and over again. Only the cells in the brain are the same through life. If these were renewed, we would lose memory. In wakefulness and in sleep, the body is renewed.

Life, which is the body's claim to reality, is temporal. But the self which says "I" is alive with another quality of being. The body, as we have said, is the house in which the self lives. The self never sleeps; only the body sleeps. But the self is alive with life eternal. The self, once born, never dies. It can be imprisoned; it can be in bonds, but its life is eternal.

If the self is truly alive, this aliveness is reflected in the body. When in Part III we travel together the five roads to man's highest destiny, we will see that the requirements are met for a healthy person in a healthy body.

## THE GIFT OF REVELATION

Always truth has been unfolding. Creation has been going on forever. The first sentence in the Bible is poetry. We read, "In the beginning God created the heaven and the earth." But God always has been. He is from everlasting to everlasting. God is the first cause. Always He has been creating. So never has there been a beginning.

Even to sense the pageantry of creation numbs us with its immensity. We cannot comprehend its magnitude; we are unable to pierce its mysteries; we can merely glimpse its splendor. When we look at nature and see its faithfulness to plan, it startles us. A tree, a delicate rose, a dandelion, the dawn and sunset; the stars in their places and the planets in their courses; the bird in flight and the fish in the sea; the elements of electrical energy in the patterns of existence—all are true to a plan.

At the center of the atom there is a nucleus of protons around which are swirling electrons moving with the precision and regularity of the planets. The spaces between them are proportionately greater than the extensions in the solar system. The laws that govern the growth of a daffodil guide the most distant star in its pathway. When we consider God's handiwork on earth, it is thrilling to realize some of the amazing facts about it.

The earth is ninety-three million miles from the sun, and the sun's rays come to us in just eight minutes. Light travels one hundred eighty-six thousand miles per second, and this is equivalent to traveling around the earth seven and one half times in one second. Even at this speed, it requires 4.3 light years for light to come to us from the nearest star. Using the astronomer's light years as a measure of distance, this 4.3 light years is twenty-six trillion miles.

We can see only a few of the nearest stars. On a clear night, where I'm writing these lines by the Gulf of Mexico, I can see perhaps 2,000 stars. This is all the Psalmist saw when he said, "The Heavens are telling the glory of God, and the firmaments proclaim His handiwork," (Ps. 19:1). But there is now talk of stars that are five hundred million, one billion, even two billion light years away. They tell us that stars are suns and each is probably the center of a solar system all its own, with planets, moons, meteors.

The earth is twenty-six thousand miles in circumference. Our sun is one hundred and ten times as big as the earth in diameter. In volume, more than a million earths are required to equal the sun. The earth, this island in space, rotates on its axis at a rate of a thousand miles an hour. It goes around the sun at approximately one and a half million miles per day. The other planets (Jupiter, for example, which is eleven times larger than the earth) rotate at varying distances from the sun and at different speeds, but all in perfect timing in relation to each other and to the sun.

Russell Shull, who is making a contribution to increased general knowledge of our universe by providing comprehensive material for our public schools, says this: "Now this little solar system of ours, with its nine planets, its thirty-one moons, and its thousands of comets is only one tiny portion of the Milky-Way which is known as our galaxy. The Milky-Way is a mighty river of suns and stars, of thousands if not millions of solar systems—all traveling through space at more than fourteen million miles a day." He continues: "And this is not all; our galaxy is one of millions of other galaxies. Within the bowl of the Big Dipper alone there are small glimmers of light which our powerful telescopes reveal to be a cluster of three hundred galaxies. . . . Astronomers now estimate there are trillions of stars within the range of our largest telescope."

Finally Mr. Shull rightly concludes, "This vision becomes too great for our minds. Time and space seem to become infinite. Some of the dim, distant galaxies of suns and stars whose light swims to our vision through two billion years do not actually exist where we see them now; that's where they were two billion years ago. It is now thought that the universe is so vast that it would take light five billion years to traverse its vastness."[2]

This is all part of the amazing revelation and gift of God. God who is infinite has created the universe that, to us, seems infinite. What is more, the creation continues, for we are told that new stars and new planets are coming into being all the time.

To look at the sky and ponder the vastness of this universe fills us with awe, but it is not the universe that we worship. God is greater than His creation. But to survey the sky, to ponder this amazing universe, is to see God in action. We look and can only say, "This is God at work."

We see order, not anarchy. And this order is not an accident; this order, this discipline, indicates infinite mind. In a consideration of the single atom or the contemplation of the entire universe (or universes!), we must be struck by this order. We cannot but feel that surely there is some vast and eternal purpose in mind—something so fabulous, so far beyond us, that we cannot fully comprehend. But one thing we can know: the way of the future is not anarchy but order, not tyranny but consent, not insanity but wholeness. What a profound resource, what a profound gift of revelation this is to us!

## THE GIFT OF THE BIBLE

Revelation comes to us not only in the amazing universe and the natural world around us, but it comes to us through the Holy Bible, for this is a major resource. It is a record of God's self-disclosure to man. It was imparted through events in the midst of war and peace and under the diversified influences of political, economic and social life. In a sense, it might be regarded as the biography of the human race through the stages of infancy, youth, adolescence and manhood. It is a drama of human life—a drama of glory when men responded to the Divine, and a drama of tragedy when human devices disregarded or ignored the manifest will of God. Viewed as history, the Bible has a continuity of thought with a steady progression toward perfection.

Just as any narrative is held together by a central theme, the Bible depends for its unity upon a continuous faith in God which inspires its diverse authors—the historians, biographers, dramatists, poets, and letter writers who sought to put into words the experiences through which they came to know God. All of them were impelled by the supreme purpose of bearing testimony to the guidance and deliverance of the wise and gracious Providence. The message of the Gospels—as old as the foundation of the world, amplified and made plain from time to time by the devotees of all religions, by saints, seers and prophets in every age—reached its highest expression and richest form in the words of the New Testament. These writers were not literary purists. They were men of deep religious concern, men who wrote things as they saw them, in the light of what they knew to be eternal realities. It is the passion of God that is unfolded in the Bible. Through its pages runs the thread of an unblemished hope for the eventual establishment of the reign of God in each human life and in the expression of collective human will.

The Christian Bible is truly the unequaled manual of religious devotion. Its promises of fellowship with God, its barest direction for the performance of duty, its many-sided program for the guidance of the individual and society, its unlimited resources for realizing the divine purpose of living, have quickened the hearts and restored the hopes of millions. The essential value of the Bible lies in its ability to encourage every individual to enter the sanctuary of personal communion with God, to receive a vivid sense of the Divine Presence in daily living.

It is a record covering twelve hundred years of spiritual searching for God, culminating in the Sermon on the Mount. In those words of Jesus we find the true pattern for living, the means of coming into the fullness of the life of the spirit, the way to life eternal. The Sermon is the eternal Gospel. The church must excite persons with a passion to achieve the life and the love that is the will of God, in order to lead them beyond a mere knowledge of the Scriptures to incorporating this knowledge into the plan and purpose of their life. When this is achieved, the Bible becomes a book of life. Alone, the Bible is the major source book of the Christian religion; it is indeed the "blue book" of life.

While the Christian road is the one that leads to the greatest fulfillment for me, there are many other roads to God, and their followers have written rich and wonderful texts which can be read by anyone who is deeply searching for truth. But the real searcher will find that all roads lead finally to the same great goal as does the Christian Bible.

## THE GIFT OF OTHER RICH RESOURCES

There are, of course, other resources—an unlimited number of devotional books, books on the life of prayer, books of spiritual biography. There are resources in the field of psychiatry and psychology, sociology, anthropology, astronomy, and the sciences of man. These rich resources are all available to us.

The moving fact is that no one needs to make a completely new beginning. Each one has the advantage of the discoveries of millions who have gone before. Among all of these gifts are great fragments of knowledge. One of the needs of the hour is to bring all of these resources together into a whole way of life for its fulfillment.

## THE PROCESSION OF GREAT SOULS

Revelation comes to us through many individuals who move across the pages of history; to read what they say, to sit at their feet, is one of the most precious experiences of life.

Some of these great figures are within the Bible; some are in other sacred books; others are great men in literature, philosophy, and the world of science. It's an impressive procession. Many of them are pioneers in the frontiers of life, carrying torches which cost lives. To enter their lives is to share in the wealth of revelation coming to us out of the past. We need to see that the past, in the deepest sense, guides us to the future.

## THE GIFT OF SCIENCE

Once there was a conflict between religion and science. In the first stage, any scientist who challenged the dogma of the church endangered his life. Remember Galileo, who came to a great insight, but had to retract it to save his life. While I believe the church provides the most saving relationship in the world, there have been many times when it was on the side of wrong.

There was a second stage when science broke free and its conflict with religion was intense. The third stage followed, when the best scientists were religious, and the best Christians were scientists. Science won one battle after another: we moved from the medicine man to scientific medicine, from offering up sacrifices to scientific agriculture. Now we're in a fourth stage, when scientists are mounting, as it were, the pulpits of the world to say, "Unless we repent, we shall likewise perish."

It is indeed interesting that a man like Bertrand Russell would say, "It is a curious fact that just as the man in the street started to put his faith in science, the scientist began to lose his faith in science."

Kirtley Mather, the geologist from Harvard, said, "The great imperative problems of our day are not in the area of chemistry or astronomy or physics, but in that of ethics and morals—something may be denoted as good will, the discerning love of the religion exemplified by Jesus."

Arthur H. Compton, who did much toward the releasing of atomic energy, says in his book *Atomic Quest*, "Within us is a still, small voice—compelling, insistent. As we listen we know that the important thing is not the state, nor the power of the atom, nor the mighty machines of industry, it is in the heart of man. To all who hear, this inner voice gives the same message because it tells that the soul of man is the true measure of values."

We live in a day when we do not want less science; we want more. My generation has lived through the most amazing scientific age. When I was born, Edison was forty-eight, Freud was thirty-nine, Henry Ford was thirty-two, Steinmetz was thirty, Madame Curie was twenty-eight, Marconi was twenty-one, Einstein was eighteen. When we stop to think, we realize that these people and others like them rendered a lasting service—gifts to heal the body, to lighten the load from shoulders, to bring help to the disturbed in mind. The finest music coming right into our homes, television and all the means of communication, transportation, the tremendous advances that have been made in every walk of life—there are not words to express the wonder of it all. There are those who feel that by 1975 we can feed as many as fifty billion people by taking water out of the sea and making it sweet, and turning deserts into gardens, taking heat from the sun, and turning the Arctic areas into fields of waving grain.

We would be supremely stupid to belittle science. Let us have more of it; let us have more pure science; let us go as far as we can in the science of man, the science of human relations. Let us go as far as we can to master human nature and set it free for the good of all men.

However, let us realize that the wonder of the contributions of these people, great as they are, are not enough. There is something wrong. There is something missing, and we know it in our hearts. When Arthur Compton was president of Washington University he made a speech to the Board of Regents. He said that as he visited with the peoples of the underdeveloped nations, he had been interested to see that they realized they must become industrialized. Yet they feared it because of what they saw in America. They see us in material prosperity, but in broken family relations, social unrest and with no clear sense of direction.

In that address, he quoted Hermann Hagedorn who, speaking of the business era of which Robert Brookings was a part, said, "It carried civilization to the vast desert areas, uncovered hidden wealth, made the American standard of living the envy of the world. The tragedy was that its triumphs, born of earth, remained true to their origin. It healed the bodies of men and trained their minds and gave their religious ceremonials expensive settings, but it did nothing to give their lives meaning or direction or to suggest that the golden apples were not the only fruit worth gathering. Rather, the spectacular harvest gave the impression that there was no other fruit; and man ate it and wondered why he starved."

## THE GIFT OF JESUS CHRIST

This leads us to realize that the supreme revelation of God is in Jesus Christ. We read, "God so loved the world that He gave His only begotten Son that whosoever believeth on Him should not perish, but have everlasting life." Jesus truly said, "I am the way, the truth and the life." Someone has well said that Jesus is the supreme event in eternity. In Part III we shall travel together the five roads to the highest destiny of man, and on the journey we shall be reminded of the deep meaning of Jesus Christ and the potential of his Lordship.

So when we stop to think of the gift of revelation, we are reminded of these words:

> We men of Earth have here the stuff
> Of Paradise—we have enough!
> We need no other stones to build
> The Temple of the Unfulfilled—
> No other ivory for the doors—
> No other marble for the floors—
> No other cedar for the beam
> And dome of man's immortal dream.

> Here on the paths of every day—
> Here on the common human way
> Is all the stuff the gods would take
> To build a Heaven, to mold and make
> New Edens. Ours the stuff sublime
> To build eternity in time.[3]

## THE GIFT OF BEAUTY

"The surpassing beauty of a sunset should not only be enjoyed; it should be recognized as the handiwork of God. A person can train himself to such a degree that sensitivity to the glories of nature automatically brings God into mind. Nature, in its myriad forms of beauty, should ever be recognized as a revelation of truth. In it we see the awe-inspiring majesty of the star firmament, the indescribable blending of color at dawn, the sinking of a flaming ball of fire into the horizon at sunset, fleecy clouds floating through the heavens, fog, rain, snow, rhododendrons, poppies, roses, an orchard at blossom time, silvery reflections on a calm lake lined with green trees, the relentless onward surge of a mighty river, the raging torrent of a mountain stream, the reverent silence of majestic trees.

"It is good for the spirit of man to experience beauty:

> Here is peace and loveliness ever mingled:
> Organ music of winds and birds and branches,
> And a brooding presence that makes each moment a
> benediction.

"Music is a conductor to fuller life. Harmony stirs the soul of man, quickens imagination, heightens aspiration and forges determination. Wise is the individual who allows time for great music, and who has trained the faculty of recognition, recognition of harmony as a revelation of God. Carl Sandburg tells of a man who went to a concert tired and discouraged and came away transformed:

> When he got outside his heels hit the sidewalk in a new way.
> He was the same man in the same world as before.

Only there was a singing fire and a climb of roses everlastingly over the world he looked on." [4]

These resources of beauty are limitless and lend infinite power. They are indeed an unfailing resource.

## THE GIFT OF NOURISHMENT

There are two kinds of nourishment, that which renews the body and that which gives wholeness to the self. How can the two be kept in a true relationship? Jesus must have had this in mind when He met with the disciples in the upper room. He took the loaf and said, "This is my body which is broken for you. Do this in remembrance of me" (1 Cor. 11:24). In memory of what? Of God breaking His body so generously that we have everything necessary for the wholeness of the body—food, clothing, shelter and renewal. And isn't it His hope that when we partake, it will be with such gratitude that we consecrate ourselves to work for a world in which all His children, all the people of the world, can win what they need for the wholeness of the body?

Then He took the cup and said, "This cup is the new testament in my blood, which is shed for you." This is in the Gospel according to St. Luke. In the Gospel according to St. John, Jesus is quoted as follows: ". . . Except ye eat the flesh of the Son of man, and drink his blood, ye have no life in you. . . . For my flesh is meat indeed, and my blood is drink indeed." Though communion is based on the chance Jesus gives us to be forgiven of our sins through Him, it has implications in terms of wholeness as well. For was not Christ suggesting that nourishment must be of the spirit as well as of the body? And was he not saying as well that it is important to maintain a balance in our utilization of various forms of nourishment? For since blood was known to Jesus as a symbol of life, he was, in effect, saying, too: "Know wholeness through my blood."

Often, when people find the heart hungry, they go on seeking more and more material goods until life has meaning only in terms of the abundance of things possessed. The struggle for existence is self-destroying unless it is dominated by spiritual visions. The desire for satisfaction of physical wants turns a desert into gardens; it sends ships across the trackless seas; it builds a marvelous industrial order. But, unless it is sanctified by the spirit of God, it makes the world a bloody battlefield and plunges society into chaos. It is never safe to go into the world crying, "Give me bread," unless one has first called, "Thy will be done." When life's supreme end becomes the achievement of God's Holy Will, then we can be trusted to make a Holy Crusade of the struggle for bread.

Today the struggle for bread and material possessions is quite real, despite the fact that we are the richest nation in the world in material things.

One hears the shout among the awakened poor with a new sense of power, "Give us bread, more bread, abundant bread; it's all our need, the end of our necessity. Take away our freedom, enslave our souls, build an insurmountable government debt in mortgages, mortgage the wages of our children's children—only make us sure of our bread and, if possible, our beer."

We build factories and cities; we make everything but men. And one day we must face the fact that we have everything but character, which can be our salvation.

It is important, therefore, that the self be nourished as well as the body. This could lead to the understanding that the struggle for bread can be a co-operative effort. Before us is the common task of subduing nature and wresting from her hands the food for our body. But so often we have attacked and fought each other instead of uniting in the work of making the earth yield in ever-increasing abundance.

When we ask ourselves what are the gifts that lift man above the level of the beast and make him indisputably different, we think of speech, art, music, writing, radio, telephones, airplanes—but isn't it plain that every one of these gifts presuppose human unity? There is something in the universe that hates walls; something that is breaking them down. This means that we must learn to love and co-operate. It is the same in industry and business. The modern way of getting bread involves a complex interdependence, and we must achieve understanding and justice and brotherhood, or see our marvelous modern system smashed to dust.

So, there is the gift of nourishment—for the body and its wholeness and for the person, that he might become whole.

And it is very important that each person realize the gift of nourishment for the body and that he take time to seek the truth that underlies physical and spiritual wholeness. This involves wise nurture.[5] And the more we come to know the truth of it, the closer we come to the achievement of wholeness.

But we need also the truth that underlies the person. We need to learn how to drink fully from the cup of life. As we come to find the truth that underlies the wholeness of the self, it is reflected in the body. This we shall see as we travel the five roads that lead to the highest destiny of the soul.

### THE GIFT OF HEALING

What a gift it is! If one pricks his finger, it heals. If a surgeon operates on a body and sews it up, what says he then? "Nature, please finish the job for me." He knows the conditions necessary for healing, but the "why" he and no one else knows.

No person in the world knows why healing takes place. Could we not say that healing—the capacity of the body and mind to regain wholeness when the appropriate conditions are met—is a natural grace? This means that no physician or surgeon or psychiatrist or priest can heal. The most they can do is to be tools in bringing about the conditions necessary for the healing to take place.

*Why does healing seem to fail?* I have seen countless persons healed in body. In fact, for a number of years in our spiritual laboratory, there was not one Service of Memory for a baby.

In my last year, I christened or dedicated two hundred and fifty-two babies but had not one Service of Memory for a baby. This is an amazing thing. There are many factors that led to this. The wonderful insights of medicine, new understandings of baby care, and perhaps something more that is beyond our words to describe.

On the other hand, I have experienced scores and scores of occasions where illness progressed until the body could no longer serve its purpose, and the spirit of the person left it. Why? This is a penetrating question.

With each of these cases I was unable to get an image of the body's wholeness—why I can't say. There are some experts in spiritual healing who feel that every body, no matter what its state, can be healed. They take this stand, for to think otherwise would seem to put limits on God.

With this position I do not agree. I believe that when God gave man the right to choose, man had to accept limitations, and that therefore there are things God cannot do. When He created law, He similarly imposed limitations. All disease is the effect of causes. Moreover, while the procreative processes are amazingly perfect, sometimes babies are born with deficiencies, such as a weak wall in a blood vessel in the brain, or an unduly small artery leading from the heart to the lungs.

Why does the healing process work in one case and not in another? In one case, the body can heal; in another, it cannot since the damage is beyond repair. The most valid spiritual healer I've ever met is Ambrose Worrel of Baltimore. Once I spent a day with him as he made hospital calls. He laid his hands on the head of a young mother with an incurable lesion. As we left the room he said to me, "Her body can't respond to healing since the damage is too great, but she is whole. She has been spiritually healed." Later, in answer to her query, I told her what he said. That evening she had a vision in which she felt she actually saw the Lord. From that time until her spirit left her body, she no longer had pain.

Others, while not healed completely, are able to go on living in the body, with limitations. One of the soundest persons I know is totally paralyzed from polio. She is whole. She has the secret of eternal life.

*There are some things we know.* One thing is certain—the person can be healed; he or she can become whole. As I've said before, I've never known a person in the ultimate moment who was not healed—who did not come into wholeness with faith to banish all fear, with freedom to love and be loved, with the grace to accept, totally.

We know, then, that the person can become whole. This being true, it may then take place in his body. If not, the person can find the grace to live with limitations. If his body cannot respond to healing, the individual can find the faith to move on without fear, in fact, with great anticipation, into the next dimension of the soul's life.

*What is the first goal?* To stay well in body. This means that each person owes it to himself to find the truth that underlies the health of the body, as we've already said.

He may find it worthwhile to join with a group in studying this truth, to turn to books and to share with others, working out a plan of life for himself. I have done this myself. Once I was in a state where drinking a glass of water gave me indigestion. Today I know the wholeness of this body and it serves me amazingly well; for this I am deeply grateful.

*What are steps in healing?* First, it is important to see the situation as it is. What is the difficulty? Is there malfunction? If there is sickness or impairment, all the facts of the condition must be learned.

This means that the first step is for the person to get a clear picture of his condition, if possible. If, however, his situation is so critical that emergency attention is necessary, his loved ones must act for him.

The second step is to see a physician. If he is wise, the physician will first listen to the patient. He will assume that the patient knows more than anyone else about himself. He then will appraise the general physical condition and study all symp toms. When he cannot be sure of a diagnosis, or if the situation obviously warrants it, he will plan for hospitalization.

Should a surgeon become involved, the third step is for the physician and surgeon to enter into teamwork. They must work together, for they have a common goal, the healing of the person.

The fourth step is the spiritual healing of the person. This will foster the physical healing as well, and hasten it. If the illness is beyond healing, then the person is ready for the ultimate. Then the important thing is whether he is whole. If whole, he will face the ultimate with courage and serenity.

The fifth step can follow naturally. If the physical healing has an emotional basis, the hidden factors can be brought to light and subsequent healing will follow. When guilt is suppressed, when other feelings are repressed, they are likely to appear as physical symptoms. When bottled-up feelings are brought to light, often the symptoms disappear.

*There is a place for a Healing Service.* There is much controversy about the Healing Service, which involves the laying on of hands. Why? Such practices can become exploitative if they are commercialized and claims are made which cannot be substantiated.

I believe in the laying on of hands. Why? The Scripture teaches it. Jesus did it. In the Book of James it is given as a clear directive. With the laying on of hands there is also the suggestion of anointing the body.

When the pastor ministers to one who is sick in body, he has a Scriptural reason to lay on hands and, if the person wishes it, to anoint the body. He does this by the authority of the Scriptures.

In like manner, the Healing Service can be held with persons coming forward to kneel at the altar. When I lay on hands, I always make it clear that healing comes through rest, through drugs, through the physician, surgeon, and dentist; it comes direct from God through another person. Then I lay on hands and say, "I am doing this because the Scriptures teach it. The healing power is infinite; pray now that I may be a clear channel, that this loved one will be free to receive the healing." In this spirit, I lay on hands.

Sometimes I suggest that the person go to the altar and kneel, knowing that the Lord is Host. Then I say, "When our Lord was in the flesh, He lay on hands and persons became whole in body and person. He is present now. Kneel and know that He lays His hands upon you, that you might be whole."

## CONCLUSION

We have shared together in the grace that is the given in life, and now we're ready to travel together the five roads that lead to the highest destiny of this person you are becoming.

# PART III. THE ROADS OF DESTINY

## CHAPTER 13. TO DAMASCUS—THE REAL SELF

A man by the name of Saul—committed to a form of religion which had lost its spirit, whose devotion was frenzied because his heart was barren, who knew what he wanted but who didn't know who he was—journeyed to Damascus. On the way, he came to know who he was by coming to know the One to Whom he belonged. Saul was the name of the illusion, the distortion, the caricature—the man who knew not himself. His name became Paul, a name for the person he was now becoming.

Was there a prelude to this? A few days before, the first martyr, Stephen, was stoned, one whose illumined soul had traveled all the roads of the highest destiny; and he said, "Lord Jesus, receive my spirit." Then as he knelt he prayed, "Lord, do not hold this sin against them." The Scripture story concludes, "And when he had said this, he fell asleep." A little earlier the record says, "Then they cast him out of the city and stoned him; and the witnesses laid down their garments at the feet of a young man named Saul" (Acts 7:58-60).

Was this not the start of Paul's awakening? Brilliant as he was, profoundly intellectual, having been taught by Gamaliel who could speak seventeen languages, highly trained in all aspects of the law, yet he must have been moved beyond logic and reason, jarred to his very depths by the revelations of Stephen, the "radar star." Even though he had authority to go to Damascus to bind up Christians and bring them back to Jerusalem, the thrust had been made. He could never be the same. Enroute he experienced God, the real God revealed in Jesus. It was a soul-shaking experience. It blinded his eyes, perhaps in wonder that he might really see and feel. He was born anew. No longer an illusion, the real self was freed from imprisonment, ready to move on to the other four roads.

For Paul this experience of coming to know who he was broke suddenly. It was a snapshot experience. For others, like Timothy, it was slower, more like a moving picture or a time exposure. I've only known a few who came to the experience of the real self quickly. In Part I we described a few. It was my experience and the experience of many, that it is slow, gradual, ongoing revelation, a growing thing. There is a time of beginning; but for some it is explosive, like a March storm; for others it is quiet and gentle, like the fluting of a summer breeze. Even for those like Paul, for whom there is a sharp suddenness, it is also an ongoing experience. All persons are born again, over and over again. The process continues in and, I think, beyond time.

What, then, are the stages of this road to Damascus? There are four.

## TO KNOW HIM TO WHOM WE BELONG

We have said that if we belong to no one, then we are cosmic accidents. If we are the crowning achievement of creation, if we, and all we can be and do, are the ultimate intent of God, then we have a high destiny; then life has real meaning.

The Prodigal Son, when living with the pigs, did not know who he was. He said, "I will arise and go to my father, and I will say to him, 'Father, I have sinned against Heaven and before you; I am no longer worthy to be called your son; treat me as one of your hired servants'" (Luke 15:18-19). But when he arrived home, he did not say it. Why? When he came to him to whom he belonged, his sonship became so plain he could no longer be a servant. His father embraced him and asked that a ring be put on his finger and shoes on his feet—all signs of royalty. Always he was a son but he did not know it. Now he was a son consciously.

Thus, the first stage to Damascus is to know God, to come to a real experience of God. But there are those who say, "How can you believe in God in a world of suffering and in a world that is moving toward nuclear suicide?" The problem of evil is a profound one, but is not the reality of good equally a puzzle? Do we not take the good for granted; but when interruption comes, when tyranny mounts, when life on this planet is in breathtaking jeopardy, then we are shocked; then we rise up and demand, "How can anyone believe in a God of love?"

One view is to see man as a victim; another is to see him as a violator of the laws of life. If we conclude that some fate or cruel absolute is responsible for suffering, tyranny, and the growth toward nuclear destruction, the outcome is hopeless. It is impossible to reform the absolute. But if man's sin is the cause—his passion to get more money, his preoccupation with comfort, his reliance on force rather than love, his lack of concern for the agony of the world—he can repent; he can come to know God, to know and love and live by the Will of God; and then there is all the hope in the world.

There are others who say God is vague; the thought of him is a blur. They say that they get nowhere in their search; they seek Him but find only a terrible sense of aloneness. This can be true for many. It was true for me. Once I knew the God of my childhood. But as I grew older, that God could no longer be acceptable to me. For I was told that if I was good, He recorded it in a book; if I was bad, He recorded that. And at the end, someone would figure out whether I would "sing or shovel." It grew upon me that if God got angry, then He was not One who could claim my complete loyalty.

The longer I looked at life, the more I knew that God had to be a God of love, that His nature was only to love. If He got angry, then I knew he was the wrong God; so I gave up that God. For some years I was agnostic. Gradually I worked my way to God analytically. I saw that there was something that made the human body. I saw a wisdom in it. I took a course in anatomy, and it became for me a moving experience. I saw a brain; I saw eyes; I saw ears; I realized the wisdom of the body. I concluded, even though it was childlike, that since man had eyes to see, something in the universe must be able to see.

But the further I went, the more I became aware that there is something in the person that says "I," for the longer I looked at human brains, the less able I was to see the thoughts of the person. I never found anyone's memory. I never saw his dreams. So it grew upon me that the body is one reality, but there is a higher reality, an existence that says "I." There is not only a creator of the human body and whatever says "I," but there is more: something that makes for fellowship. These things I could see; these things I could accept.

Gradually I grew to feel that there was a power greater than I had ever known. I began to study Jesus, to do what He said, to make a study of the life of prayer. I began to pray, and continued even if it left me cold. Now and then I broke through and came to a sense of God. To follow Jesus and to do what He says and to pray, proved valid. I began to read the Bible and other religious books. I began to organize small research groups, in which I was a fellow searcher. For a time I found reality, and then again I lost it. I went through dry periods. These seemed to me to have two meanings; dry periods were my original state, and in my later life, I felt maybe God withdrew from me for my own good, that I might seek harder and with more sincerity.

At the same time, I saw others search, some making progress easily, others with greater difficulty. A brilliant young man came with our college people to be silent for a half hour a day in our sanctuary, but was making no headway. Sometimes he became very impatient, but he kept coming. Months later, he rushed to me at the close and said, "I've found a little bit of peace." It was a breakthrough.

Today he is a brilliant surgeon. Now and then I see him and ask, "How is it with you?"

"I'm finding a little more peace," he has said. "And what is more, increasingly I operate with the sense that the wisdom involved in the operation of the universe, the wisdom out of which came this amazing reality that is the human body, is available to me as a surgeon. I am so glad that I spent those months in the sanctuary, for now I know that as a doctor my first job is with the person, my second with his body."

There are two things we must understand if we are to know God. First, we cannot see Him, as no one can really see you. You have one thing in common with God: neither He nor you can be truly seen, but you can be experienced by others. Moreover, what we do not see may be more meaningful than what we do see. The great persons I have known became sure of God; their faith was pillared upon their soul's fellowship with Him. The young surgeon kept coming to the sanctuary, almost desperately. One night he emerged confident. He had not found a complete explanation of life, but God became real to some degree. It was a high moment in his journey to Damascus.

I say again, the greatest men of the world, the human mountain peaks, came to know deep in their hearts that they were not on their own.

One day, as I read the Bible, I found that the writer of Hebrews is confident that we are not alone. He talks about a man who, by a stroke of favor, found himself within reach of a great throne, a place of leadership in a mighty empire. But this man turned away from it to become the leader and inspiration of a band of runaway slaves. This man, who is thought by many to be one of the greatest minds who ever lived, did this daring thing, even though he was to know hardship and poverty and the base ingratitude of those for whom he had forsaken all. By the sheer power of his soul, he had to communicate courage and hope to his daring followers. Above all, he was constrained to see them betray the religious faith, the freedom and destiny of which had impelled him to lead them forth in search of a new home. And now, as the writer of Hebrews looks back over the romance and heroism of that consecrated life, he sees not one thing in his environment or in his comradeship that can

account for his courage. What made him go on? Where was the
hidden power? From what secret spring did he refresh and ener-
gize his soul? He reached the conclusion in these words: "Moses
endured as seeing Him that is invisible" (Heb. 11:27). He was
a man who lived and acted as if he saw what cannot be seen, yet
can be so richly known. He did such great work because he was
not alone, because he got his directions straight and started toward Damascus.

Unlike this writer, there are those who assert a great belief in
man and the possibilities of the rich life he will yet develop
and the kingdom of kindness he will yet erect, who maintain
the humanistic point of view, who assume there is no God. Anyone who asserts such a belief and builds his life upon it, is involved in an act of religious faith. What makes us believe that
man in the future will become more spiritual than the ends he
seeks? Who gave us to believe that humanity is on its upward
road? Men as acute and honest as many of the humanists I know,
cannot find the evidence in history. Under the shadow of the
greatest peril which ever faced man, the peril of nuclear warfare—when man was never so adequate and yet never so frightened—it is nothing less than a great affirmation of faith to believe
in a mankind that is to be. In other words, men such as these, in
order to support life at all and give it any creative content, live
as though they believe that purpose is inherent in life, even
though their philosophy denies it. No man can live nobly in a
purposeless universe. If he believes in no divine purpose, he will,
out of his own aspiration, create meaning for life and live as
though it had the universe supporting it. We can only endure
in the high enterprise of the soul when we sense Him who is
invisible.

When, in our own lives, we seek love and goodness, disciplined
and guided by intelligence, there comes a conviction that we're
not alone. Indeed, we find that such aspiration is not ours alone,
but that we have entered into the mighty purpose of the universe.
There is born a sense of companionship, and in the hearts of
those most completely consecrated, a peace that passeth all under-

standing. Passionately putting meaning into life, they have found meaning there. The great support of love and sacrifice and heroism is the belief that those inspiring qualities which we find here and there in human souls are not just broken, stray beams of light, but come from a mighty sun. All you must do to believe in God is to believe that the highest and most humane qualities you possess are not only in you, but in the universe. There is not only personal validity, but cosmic significance as well. As a bit of electrical energy and a piece of magnetized steel tell of oceans of electrical energy, so the love and goodness of the human heart are not isolated phenomena; they tell us of One who is the soul and source of all goodness. And so man hears and takes heart; he knows the visions of his soul are valid. Life is no accident. Somewhere it has abiding significance, and man endures by sensing Him who is invisible.

The religion that has given man a vision of sovereign God has inspired a faith that releases great heroism in its followers. Such religion has been a strange stimulus; under its power men have thrown their lives away for causes that seemed to be lost and for tasks that seemed impossible to achieve. They were stoned, they were torn asunder. They were tempted, they were slain with the sword, they went about in sheepskin and goatskin, destitute, afflicted, ill-treated, falling in deserts and holes in the earth, men of whom the world was not worthy—but they received not the promise.

Today we need to remember that the greatest human adventures have risen from the hearts of men who walked with God. More than one American historian has said that democratic ideals are a by-product of religious faith.

I have a great desire to go to Geneva, Switzerland, where stands a famous sculptured group. I am told that in the midst stands John Calvin, austere reformer, with soul aflame with thoughts of God's sovereignty; close to him stands William the Silent of Holland; there is Admiral Coligny of France; here is John Knox of Scotland, yonder a Pilgrim father of New England and there, Oliver Cromwell—all champions of free government but first of all, Christians. You look at these men and you cannot say that religion is an opiate of the people. Religion an opiate? There is a fine irony in that phrase, coming from a party or creed that conscripts men's minds by controlling what they shall read, censoring what they shall hear, and drugging atmosphere with falsehood.

"Religion is the opiate of the people." The communists who use that slogan to express their religious philosophy might be surprised to know that it was not originated by Karl Marx. He cribbed it from a devoted follower of Jesus and one of the most effective ministers who ever lived—Charles Kingsley. But Kingsley used it to refer to the formalism and ethical lethargy of the church of his day.

The men represented in the sculpture, and millions like them, including those who conceived our democratic way of life, got their inspiration from the open Bible. They marched to the music of a great imperative. Halford Luccock once said that the word "imperative" may have about it the drag of chains or the lift of wings. "We must obey God rather than men," was said in the reckless exultation of a great conviction; it was not an agonized admission wrung from the heart. If we are to endure in our search for wholeness, if goodness and truth and human freedom are to be maintained in a world darkened by the fog of secularism, we must see with the eyes of faith an invisible God in the shadow of whose glory we live and in whose fellowship is all our joy. If we are to prevent a society in which men would rather be rich slaves than poor freemen, we must recapture the conviction that we were born to be the sons of God.

Just as we cannot completely define a symphony or a sunset, we cannot fully comprehend the nature of God. We need to recall our first guiding principle: faith is reason grown courageous. One day it may become knowledge.

Life's enduring values are known, not through conquest or acts of will, but through surrender. Thus we may become the vehicle of a higher beauty in truth and goodness. The sheer romance of earthly existence, the mystery and glory of it, is in the fact that God's spirit seeks to live in human life, and that we may become vessels, sanctified and fit for His use. It is only into the humble and surrendered soul that the spirit of beauty may come. We cannot know the power of a Dresden Madonna or a Fifth Symphony except in self-surrender, by which our souls become plastic in the hands of beauty. A great artist, when asked if, in his highest moments of ecstatic insight, he felt he was using his own power or being used by a higher power, replied, "It is both, but much more the latter. I am the obedient servant of a beauty that is ever seeking to express itself in concrete forms." Is it not true that eternal goodness seeks humble and contrite hearts in which to dwell? All the problems of life, its success or failure, are met by the surrender of self. "We cannot," says Chesterton, "think too little of ourselves and we cannot think too much of our souls."

The experience of God, no matter what the religion through which it is mediated, always strikes a soul with two convictions. First, there is an awareness of unconditional demand; the soul must make a surrender. Second, there is the consciousness that the highest well-being of the soul is bound up in obedience to that demand. The selfish man comes one day to be no self; there is nothing but the perpetual clash of contradictory desires. On a memorial tablet in Oxford erected to Richard Lewis Nettleship, may be read these words, "He loved great things and thought little of himself; desiring neither fame nor influence he won the devotion of men and was a power in their lives." In the deepest sense, he was more than a conqueror.

Success that does not go beyond conquest, beyond aggressive effort on our part, is often a threat and not a promise. This does not mean that we do not adventure, that there isn't a place for conquest, but the mistake is in believing that to be a conqueror is all that matters. We've spoken before of conquering nature and making it serve our ends. This we have done in an almost magical manner. Our hands are full of the spoils of battle; the fruits of conquest are everywhere. We are a generation of conquerors, and yet we are impotent, fear-ridden people who can do nothing to save ourselves and our civilization from ruin. We have made many conquests but have failed to dedicate them to spiritual ends. To a great degree, we have kept the spirit of the conqueror supreme, and now our conquests threaten our very existence.

When Thoreau was asked to admit that a train going thirty miles an hour represented an advance over the stagecoach, he said, "No, of course not, if it is only the chance for a mean man to go faster." What is the use of all our conquests of disease if we are to perish in nuclear warfare; what good is the conquest of the air if its principal use is to drop bombs on defenseless people? Do the motion pictures and television represent any real progress if they are the means to communicate attitudes that make people sick? We need to see that there is a vast difference between civilization and culture. Gadgets and devices represent civilization, but unless they are used to serve spiritual ends they do not mean culture. Civilization will die; it is only culture that survives. Civilization is achieved by the conqueror. Culture comes to and through those who are more than conquerors, those who have learned to surrender to the holy God. The only hope for our civilization is that its conquerors shall bring the results of their victory and bow before Him whose love can transform our lives and our goals.

Stumbling up a lonely hill one day, I had a vision. I saw a cross-laden man. When he reached the crest, they nailed him to his cross. Far back in the shadows stood Alexander and Hannibal and Pilate, Judas, Herod and Tiberius, all of whom expressed scorn and pity. They said, "This man might have been a success; he might have been a conqueror. Now he hangs there a broken victim—lonely, friendless and forgotten." But they did not see; they could not know He chose to be more than they. For no conqueror could redeem your soul and mine. He had to surrender to God, in order that we might come to know Him and follow Him. And it is only by surrendering our very best to Him and His will that we become persons true to our highest destiny.

## TO RECOVER THE FREEDOM TO GROW

This is the second stage in the road. The child is free to grow, but many men and women lose this capacity. Somehow they no longer desire to know and respond to truth. But those who do, know that the experience of God is a profound awakening. The heart becomes open, the mind becomes teachable. This does not always happen quickly; some must search patiently and diligently. When I committed myself to the life of prayer, I said, "I'll keep on if it kills me, for I'm going to learn prayer-power." I kept at it through long dry periods. In time, however, I found the truth of one of the principles stated in Chapter 1, "I had to accept the discipline of duty to know its delight."

So the freedom to grow comes from God's gift to us and our intense effort. The result is that we become free to confess the wrong we have done and the good we have not done; we repent; we know that we are forgiven, so we can forgive; we make restitution for the harm we have done in the past. And we maintain the freedom to deal with the failures of the future.

Moreover, with this freedom to grow, the readiness to be taught, and a hunger for the truth, we can not only get to Damascus but take the other four roads.

## TO UNDERSTAND THE PERSON WE ARE

This is the third stage on the way to Damascus. We not only come to a sense of our sonship of God; we come to understand ourselves, which makes it possible to understand those around us.

You will grow into understanding of yourself by studying the Scriptures, especially the Gospels. You will find it valuable to observe your reactions to other persons—those who are aggressive, those who expect sympathy, the grateful and the ungrateful, the loving and the bitter, the domineering and the passive. Notice if you react defensively or with understanding; whether you have a need to judge with condemnation or with compassion; whether you suffer excessively or are indifferent.

You may find it valuable to seek a person with whom you feel free to talk and whose wisdom you find helpful. Moreover, participation in a research group can be of unlimited value, as we said in Chapter 3. In Part IV we shall describe in detail a group relationship that can lead to wholeness.

A check list such as the following may be of real value. Just sit quietly and consider these questions, answering as you can:

1. Am I governed by long-range plans, or am I the victim of impulses and shifting moods?

2. Can I grant others the right to be what they are and accept them in those terms, or do I project my feelings onto them and try to make them over as I want them?

3. How do I react to the authority of others? Do I rebel, or do I submit, either with strong feelings or passively?

4. Can I stand on my own convictions quietly and with deep confidence?

5. Can I maintain control of my choices against inner impulses or against onslaughts from without?

6. Can I accept sexual desire as a great gift and fit it into a plan of life? Can I work with the opposite sex without getting emotionally involved? Can I focus my total mate-love on one person of the opposite sex?

7. Can I withdraw from labor, shifting gears so that I may enjoy recreation without a sense of guilt?

8. In the relationships of love, on a friend, parent and mate basis, do I need persons because I love them or do I love them because I need them?

9. Am I able to give myself and others the right to make mistakes?

10. In experiences where there is a difference of opinion, can I hear the other person clearly and fully?

11. In dealing with negative feelings in others, do I react from their viewpoint or from mine?

12. Am I able to learn everything I can from a mistake or

failure or embarrassment, and then wrap it up and go on?

13. Am I able to accept myself in my work and family roles and work for ongoing growth?

14. Do I have a persistent desire to know?

15. Am I co-operative or a solo player?

16. Am I friendly? Am I compassionate or self-centered?

17. Do I live by consent, or do I coerce others?

18. Can I take criticism, or am I defensive?

19. Am I critical of others, or am I understanding?

20. Am I slow to condemn, or am I quick to pass judgment?

21. Do I feel confident, or am I anxious?

22. Do I live by faith, or am I plagued by fear?

23. Am I impulsive, or am I objective?

24. Is prayer a way of life for me?

25. Do I act out of love or because I feel I "should"?

26. Am I free to love, or are my feelings blocked?

27. Do I feel that I am happily married?

28. Do I find contentment and satisfaction in my work?

29. Is God real to me, or is He vague?

30. Do I focus on health or on sickness?

31. Do I feel close to people, or do they seem distant?

32. Do I love the church, or do I attend out of habit?

33. Do I seek to follow Jesus, or do I tend to live as I please?

34. Do I ignore those who do not have a white skin?

35. Am I a leader, or am I only aware of my weaknesses?

36. Do I try to work for conditions which will foster peace, or do I feel that war is inevitable?

37. Am I thrilled with life, or am I confused?

38. Am I frank with others, or do I withhold my feelings?

39. Do I say what I think, or do I talk behind the other person's back?

40. Do I set aside time for study and meditation?

To ponder questions such as these undoubtedly helps each one of us to come to know where he is.

## *TO COME TO KNOW THE PERSON YOU CAN LOVE*

This is the last stop before Damascus. You know who you are; you become teachable; you grow in understanding of yourself, and you know the person you can love. You say, "How can I love myself; is this not selfish?" The answer is "no." The selfish person hates himself and is preoccupied with himself. But if you know the person you can love, you no longer focus on yourself but become a channel of love. Did Jesus not say, "Love your neighbor as yourself"? When we know the person we can love we are made alive in the process. Life is now expressing itself through us. People around us are becoming whole.

Who is the person you can love? The real self, the central core that is *you*, the Christ-self, the child of God. It is your nature to love. If you hate, you will get sick and make others sick. If you love, you will be whole and others in your circle of fellowship will become whole. But wholeness will grow beyond you and your circle, until it reaches around the world. When this happens, you're ready to start on the road to Jericho.

## *LET US CONSIDER THE VIEWS OF TWO PERSONS*

Walt Whitman, a man with an extra dimension to his mind, has some interesting thoughts. He sees the glory of being a "simple separate person." The miracle of existence seemed to him the greatest of wonders. He felt that to be able to love oneself is a supreme achievement necessary to self-fulfillment. While Whitman loved himself, he always made it clear that one of the conditions of self-love was the love of others. When he celebrated his own existence, he celebrated that of all human beings: "Whoever walks a furlong without sympathy, walks to his own funeral drest in his shroud."

He says, in utter beauty and with dynamic power:

"I am the man, I suffer'd, I was there.
The disdain and calmness of martyrs,
The mother of old, condemn'd for a witch, burnt with dry
    wood, her children gazing on,
The hounded slave that flags in the race, leans by the fence,
    blowing, cover'd with sweat,
The twinges that sting like needles in legs and neck,
    the murderous buckshot and the bullets,
All these I feel or am . . .
Agonies are one of my changes of garments.
I do not ask the wounded person how he feels, I myself
    become the wounded person . . .
Behold I do not give lectures or a little charity,
When I give I give myself."[1]

Dr. Viktor Frankl, in *The Doctor and the Soul,* makes this
matter of self-love very clear. "If it is a virtue to love my neighbor as a human being, it must be a virtue—and not a vice—to
love myself, since I am a human being too. There is no concept of man in which I myself am not included. A doctrine
which proclaims such exclusion proves itself to be intrinsically
contradictory . . ."[2]

## CONCLUSION

The road to Damascus leads to the real self—one who knows
who he is, who is free to care for his failures and to seek knowledge and wisdom, who grows in self understanding, who comes
to know the person he can love, and who is a channel of love.
Arriving at Damascus, one is ready to start toward Jericho.

# CHAPTER 14. TO JERICHO—COMPASSION

No one can get to Jericho if he by-passes Damascus. When he comes to know the person he can love; when he is a channel of love—only then can he find his way to Jericho.

In the 10th Chapter of Luke we find one of the greatest stories ever told, "And behold, a lawyer stood up to put him to test, saying, 'Teacher, what shall I do to inherit eternal life?' He said to him, 'What is written in the law? How do you read?' And he answered, 'You shall love the Lord your God with all your heart, and with all your soul, and with all your strength, and with all your mind; and your neighbor as yourself.' And He said to him, 'You have answered right; do this, and you will live.'

"But he, desiring to justify himself, said to Jesus, 'And who is my neighbor?' Jesus replied, 'A man was going down from Jerusalem to Jericho, and he fell among robbers, who stripped him and beat him, and departed, leaving him half dead. Now by chance a priest was going down that road; and when he saw him he passed by on the other side. So likewise a Levite, when he came to the place and saw him, passed by on the other side. But a Samaritan, as he journeyed, came to where he was; and when he saw him, he had compassion, and went to him and bound up his wounds, pouring on oil and wine; then he set him on his own beast and brought him to an inn, and took care of him. And the next day he took out two denarii and gave them to the innkeeper, saying, 'Take care of him; and whatever more you spend, I will repay you when I come back.' Which of these three, do you think, proved neighbor to the man who fell among the robbers? He said, 'The one who showed mercy on him.' And Jesus said to him, 'Go and do likewise'" (Luke 10:25-37).

How often we have heard this story! But how much has it influenced our behavior? The good Samaritan came to where the man was. This was the first important fact. Two other men, leaders in the religion of the day, who never got to Damascus, went by on the other side. The Samaritan—traditional enemy of the Jews—did not pass by. He came to the wounded man, bound up his wounds and took him to the inn. He not only paid the innkeeper, but said, "Take care of him and whatever more you spend, I will repay you when I come back."

This man had surely been to Damascus. He came to where the man was; he had compassion; he expressed it in a very tangible way.

## GOD AND MAN IN ACTION

The man who has been to Damascus knows a relationship in which he becomes a co-creator with God. God's real glory is man. All other living things are set in the precision of instinct. Their behavior is determined by inbred forces and directives. There is no choice, only pure response to pure stimuli. But man is free to choose. His freedom is not absolute, but it is real.

We are in an unfinished world. We could not stand a finished world, for we would have nothing to do. God elevates us to the supreme relationship by which we can help finish His world. We enter into a cosmic teamwork and miracles happen; the impossible becomes possible.

## THIS ROAD MUST BECOME A THOROUGHFARE

When a person travels with clear vision and open heart and mind to Jericho, he can meet the requirements for friendship, love, marriage, parenthood, and vocational fulfillment. He is able to be a member of a team which strives to build community, to turn the tide from war to peace, and to push back the barriers of tyranny until men everywhere know freedom. But to our doom, this is not usually the case. Marriage so often is a relationship of people who find each other physically but not spiritually, leaving the heart famished. In such a relationship there is neither understanding nor compassion.

Parents must reach their children with compassion and understanding. We know that if babies are not given tender, loving care they tend to withdraw into themselves. This can stunt their growth and cause them to lose their hold on life to such an extent that they become sick, even to the point of death.

The same concern must be shown by the physician, the employer, the teacher, the public servant, the neighbor, the world citizen. Without this we are doomed. The same is true, for example, in the church. I see few churches where people reach out to others with compassion. The same is desperately true in our high schools, where one-third of the students are unwanted and rejected by their fellow students. Many persons are either withdrawn or full of rage; but for millions more, life is empty, devoid of meaning.

In every community there are to be found the rejected, the deserted, the poor, the lonely, the handicapped—persons who are so limited by circumstances, nature, or themselves, that they contemplate the future with little hope.

Those more favored give a little to the United Appeals but in the giving they never reach these enslaved persons caught in the ghetto of economic, cultural, and vocational limitation. Those who could help never go to the needy ones. So crime mounts; sickness grows; our way of life breaks down.

Think of our jails and penitentiaries, our mental institutions and those who care for limited people! Ponder how many persons are unaware, who never give a thought to those in want and despair. Most of them are in this condition because they were not loved; there is hope for them only if they are loved.

## WE NEED TO UNDERSTAND RELIGION

True religion is a way of life for those who have been to Damascus and who then head for Jericho. Is it not important for us to see that, in a sense, religion is an art? Its great appeal is to the emotions. Its deep beginnings are in a world that transcends human relations. For through religion the human spirit can find fellowship with the eternal; man can know a cosmic comrade in whose fellowship the soul's loneliness is banished.

But how can this experience be known? There is only one way: it must be known as the beauty of art is known—through imagination and contemplation, through opening the soul to the Infinite; through responding to God's revealing until one comes within the circle of divine harmony. This power comes not from action, but through being still and knowing God. Never does the human spirit know such joy, such uplift, and aliveness, as it can know in union with God.

The way to this supreme experience is not primarily through doing the highest we know; rather it comes by way of intense awareness, wishful wonder, and full surrender. There is a supposed saying of Jesus, omitted by the four Evangelists but attested to by many of the church fathers, including Clement of Alexandria: "Wonder at the things before you." We can believe Jesus said it when we recall his words, "Unless you turn and become like children, you will never enter into the kingdom of heaven" (Matt. 18:3).

In prayer, the person is seeking to come to know God, that he may know the person he can love. Its highest expression is adoration. It is the mobilization of the soul's highest powers. It demands inner cleansing and growing awareness. Man prays alone and in fellowship. Often his best research and achievement of prayer power will be found in fellowship. He needs this hour of worship when he joins with others in prayer. Long ago, when persons joined in common worship, they sought settings of beauty, mystic symbolism, and the truth revealed in music and Scripture. Even in personal prayer and meditation, music, a cross, or some other token, are of great worth. So in this regard, religion is a supreme art.

But religion is also conduct. It is doing right. Someone said, "My religion is living the Golden Rule." Long ago the prophet

Amos came to a temple of worship and, speaking in the name of God, cried, "I hate, I despise your feasts, and I take no delight in your solemn assemblies. Even though you offer me your burnt offerings and cereal offerings, I will not accept them, and the peace offerings of your fatted beasts I will not look upon. Take away from me the noise of your songs; to the melody of your harps I will not listen. But let justice roll down like waters, and righteousness like an everflowing stream" (Amos 5:21-24).

The prophet might be speaking to the church today, which is so strong in word but so weak in practice. If one really prays, the fruits of superior conduct will distinguish his life. He prays as he goes to Damascus and then, surely, he will head toward Jericho.

Obviously, if we love not man whom we can experience, how can we love God who is invisible to us? But if religion is only morality, beginning and ending in man, then its lifeblood does not flow and the center of the universe is not God. If all the goodness of the universe begins and ends in man, if he alone cares for righteousness, when he ceases to be, all the values of the universe are nothing more than dust.

Religion is neither art alone nor ethics alone; it is a wonderful blend of both. It is the heart's highest response to God, expressed in great conduct; it is the soul's vision, making itself known in human relations. The inner experience is the soul; the outer experience is the body. One without the other is either a ghost or a corpse.

Real religion is love, intense and passionate and consuming; religion is conduct, beautiful and clean, but conduct that arises out of the vision of God, out of the implication of the soul's communion with Him.

## THE REQUIREMENTS OF THE ROAD TO JERICHO

We must practice reaching out to others. As I walked the prayer path, I began to go to people, to listen to them, to hear them, to see them. The more I could come to know the person

I could love, the more I could reach out to others and identify with understanding and compassion.

I went to the places in our city where suffering abounded. I made a practice of going to our mental institutions, to rest homes, to our workhouses and to the penitentiary. Once someone questioned me about my "compulsion" to visit such places —particularly the penitentiary. I told him in all honesty, "I go because I don't want to lose God."

In *The Devil's Advocate*, there is a striking section about a priest who, facing the ultimate moment, lacked the faith he preached to others. He had intellectually ascribed to the power of religion—the package he was trained to sell—but he was without the deep conviction of faith. Finally he was advised to go to a poor parish where he could walk the ways of men and thus find for himself the faith he advocated.

Enroute to his new parish, a fellow priest summed up his problem in these words, "There is no passion in your life, my son. You have never loved a woman, nor hated a man, nor pitied a child. You have withdrawn yourself too long and you are a stranger in the human family. You have asked nothing and given nothing. You have never known the dignity of need nor gratitude for our suffering shared. This is your sickness. This is the cross you have fashioned for your own shoulders. This is where your doubts began and your fears too—because a man who cannot love his fellows cannot love God either."[1]

I had to go out and bear witness to the agony of the world. I had to stand where I could hear the cry of the hungry children of the world. I came to know that if I could not hear them, I could not hear God, nor could I hear you, the reader. I began to read, to talk to nationals from other countries. In my meditative life I became receptive to God and also to persons near and far. I tried with all my heart to hear them, and one night I had a moving experience. I went to the University Hospital in Columbus and as I entered, I heard a baby cry. I went over to a couple with a very young baby. I said to them, "Is there something I can do?"

"No, the baby's hungry," the mother replied.

Then I became personal and said, "Why don't you feed it?"
"It's not time," she answered.

Then I became really personal and said, "Well, who knows better, the clock or the baby's stomach?"

She must have been to Damascus. She must have been well on the way to Jericho, for she looked up and smiled and said, "You have a point; where can I heat this milk?"

I led her to the coffee shop and, after introducing her to the hostess, I went to the eleventh floor to minister to someone. On returning to the lobby, I heard the greatest silence that ever settled over the earth—the silence that follows the cry of a hungry baby now being fed. I stood and watched the wonderful sight of a contented baby.

I turned to leave and on the way out, believe it or not, I heard. I had prayed for a long time that I might hear the hungry children of the world. That night I heard them faintly. It shook me to my very depths, and I've never been the same since. My wife and I have been in the process of revising our budget ever since.

We must know that food is the major problem facing our world. Each night one half of the world's people go to bed hungry. Food is the greatest weapon in the cold war. Who knows this better than the communists? It is interesting that Khrushchev promises that the Soviets will produce abundant food in the future—always in the future.

But our problem, unlike Russia's and Red China's, is not scarcity but overabundance. Our food surpluses have become unmanageable. There is hunger and famine in every area, wherever we are in conflict with the communists—throughout Asia, Africa, South America. The miracle of our methods of producing food, if adapted to local situations, would bring a world-wide revolution. With it would come other gains in terms of a growing world market which would bless us as it blesses others.

We have technical skills that no people ever had before. We not only have bread, but forty million Americans each own one car; 6,350,000 have two cars. More than fifty million families have refrigerators. We spend millions each year on chewing gum.

On the other hand, in 1960, due to decreases in China's harvest, food production in the world gained only one per cent, while population increased 1.6 per cent. Two-thirds of the population of the world go to bed hungry, and the peoples of Asia, Africa and South America are plagued by disease. People have a right to live. This is an eternal right. But people also have a right to a sense of being and the opportunity to fulfill their lives with excellence. A startling fact is that one-third of the adults of the world can't read. Illiteracy runs as high as eighty-five per cent in some countries. In 1960, Edward R. Murrow said: "In Africa, with a population of over two hundred thirty-six million people, newspapers reach less than three million persons. In the Far East, with a population of seven hundred sixty-seven million, newspapers reach only one and one-third per cent of the people."

It is not enough to be anticommunist. We will never whip communism simply by fighting it. This can only be accomplished by encouraging and propagating a superior way of life. We need to be pro-people and freedom.

But we can best help others by helping them to help themselves. In this way, love and restraint are mingled together. There are wonderful agencies through which we can work: World Neighbors of Oklahoma City; Agricultural Missions, 475 Riverside Drive, New York City; Church World Service, 475 Riverside Drive, New York City; Agricultural Aids, Los Angeles. Through such channels we can share our skills. We do not simply give things; we share the secret of knowledge so that others may come to know who they are and gain their rightful sense of dignity.

## THERE IS NO OTHER WAY TO SURVIVAL

If we can make our way to Jericho, we can begin to turn the tide from war to peace. Sometimes one almost wonders whether the death wish, so often dominant in the deep self, is not at the heart of the human condition. Are men so fascinated with the face of death, that they have lost their power to choose life, and meet the requirements for its fulfillment in the world under law? Sometimes we seem indeed to be in a crisis out of which we do not know how to negotiate ourselves, caught in a momentum toward war which we cannot change.

As we move toward Jericho, we begin to be the peacemakers. We are told in the New Testament Beatitude, "Blessed are the peacemakers for they are the sons of God." We become sensitive; we begin to build bridges; we become persons through whom God can fulfill His purpose. The tide not only can be turned from war to peace, but the barriers of tyranny can be broken down until all men are free.

# CHAPTER 15. TO EMMAUS—SPIRITUAL UNION

The third road to man's highest destiny leads to Emmaus. Two men were enroute to this city several days after the Crucifixion and the revelation of Easter morning. They were joined by a stranger. As they went along the road, they talked of the events of the previous day. The record says that "their hearts burned within them."

At the day's end, the two invited the stranger to tarry with them, and as they broke bread together, they recognized him to be the Resurrected Christ.

They knew kinship. They became close, especially in the breaking of bread. The two men found union with each other and with Jesus. Surely they had been to Damascus and to Jericho, or they never would have been able to reach Emmaus.

To journey toward Emmaus, one must know who he is, understand who he is, and know the person he can love. Then he can express deep concern for the other person, no matter what his state of being, no matter what his station in life. He can reach out to him with compassion, be he white, black or yellow, be he sensitive or insensitive, be he religious or agnostic. Then he is on his way to Emmaus, where he can love and be loved, to join in deep spiritual union with another and with God.

## THE MEANING OF LOVE

No one can fully explain love. The Bible says that God is love. We touched on this when we said there is a power in life that makes for fellowship. Alfred North Whitehead, the great philosopher, pointed out that there is a plan at work in the universe. I think we would certainly agree that this plan was at work before man entered the drama of life. Many great thinkers have been calling our attention to this plan. General Smuts refers to it as a "whole-making process." In it he sees something which is creating ever more "complex wholes."[1] Whitehead refers to it as a process of concretion—something which is making actual more aspects of reality in one event.[2] Lloyd Morgan envisions a force which is stimulating the emergence of higher levels of life.[3] Wieman sees an "increase of mutuality," a "process of integration" going on in the world.[4] Montagu sums up the thoughts of these great minds when he says, "And so we are confronted with a God that exists, not as an omnipotent monarch, a giver of laws and punishment, but as an ascending force, nisus, a thrust toward concentration, organization and life. This power appears to labor slowly and under difficulty. We can liken it to a yeast that, through the eons, pervades the chaos of matter and slowly leavens it with spirit."[5]

Dr. Whitehead feels that the tiny energy centers appear, at first glance, to be feeding on each other, but a more careful examination indicates they're cooperating with each other, or making for mutuality. There is something in a person which inevitably draws him to other people. We see this early in all stages of developing life, whether among animals or among human beings. We see a group of boys forming into a fellowship to do things that sustain each other. We see girls establish friendships, and children form cliques or groups. We see a fundamental friendship grow between two boys or between two girls. When the proper time comes, we see a boy, drawn in a strange but beautiful and meaningful way to a girl; and we see a girl respond to some inner yearning which links her to the boy. Then, if we continue to watch, we may see the relationship develop into the companionship of love and become so binding that it reaches into the sunset of their togetherness.

Is it not true, therefore, that this force in the universe which makes for mutuality and fellowship, has laid a fundamental plan which gives us a clue to the nature of God? Here is, for example, a home with a father and mother and three children. The minute you step into that home, you sense a fellowship that is very real. All the members of the family help to sustain that fellowship and all are sustained by it. As you move in that fellowship for a time, you discover there something more than personality. You discover personalities living creatively together. Sometimes I feel that the universe has been developed not only to create personality, but to achieve those values that result when personalities live creatively together. In this family, for example, is a spirit which is a personality in itself; it is distinctive, for you can isolate it by its very nature. Doesn't that give us a little clue as to God's nature? He is all that persons can be in themselves. He is the process out of which persons are born and within which they grow individually, but He is also everything they can achieve in their creative togetherness. Of course, He is more than this, but it is a partial understanding of His nature.

So God is ever bringing together. Love unites and makes whole. Hate divides, disintegrates, and destroys. God is love in the sense that He is ever bringing all life to fulfillment.

Moreover, God is ever giving. The given in life, when sensed even to a small degree, is beyond the power of words to describe. God is the source of life. He *is* life in that He is the giver, the sustainer, the renewer of life. He gave to each of us being and infinite possibilities of becoming.

The plan of creation, infinite and abounding in wonders, is part of the given—the behavior of the electron, the unfolding of the daffodil, the conception, birth and growth of all living things, the stars and planets in their courses, and all the resources for unlimited achievements in the union of God and man.

Across the millennia, there have been countless persons who got to the cities of human destiny and added their contribution to the great common wealth. We are infinitely richer because of their devotion to the highest they knew.

Some years ago a young woman, who was then youth director

in our Spiritual Fellowship,[6] planned a service of worship, using ideas from a legend of Olive Shriner. The service left all of us with a lasting memory and with new appreciation of the gift of those who have gone before. The details I no longer remember, but the lesson remains vivid. As I recall, it was a story of ants trying to cross a small stream. One after another was carried away, but thousands came, some catching onto a stick or a twig. Finally, there were so many that a dam was formed, and in time others crossed over on the sacrificed bodies of those who went before.

The lesson is plain. The pioneers of the race go into the stream, face the hazards, and keep true to some tyrant dream of truth. They give their bodies as living sacrifices and become a bridge over which succeeding generations pass. In their day, they may have been hated and maligned. In time they become more than a bridge; they are heroes, human mountain peaks to which millions look for inspiration and instruction. They are, to change the figure, "radar stars" in the sky of the present and of the future.

God's gift is especially transforming and redemptive in the Old Testament prophets, the saints and sinners of all the roads to the spiritual summit. But His supreme gift to millions is Jesus of Nazareth, who is for us God's human face.

God's love not only brings union; it is not only expressed in the given of life; it is within us. God loves us totally. It is His nature to love. His supreme concern is that each person will know His love and will love Him with all their mind, heart and soul and their neighbor as themselves. His every thought, His infinite grace, His total being centers on the becoming of each person in the fulfillment which is the intent of all creation.

He gives totally and He seeks constantly to be known in us and through us. We can never get away from His love. If we go to hell, it is there; if we go to Heaven, it is there; if we travel on the wings of the morning or dwell beneath the sea, it is there. His love fills the universe. Whenever and wher-

ever a man opens his heart, there is God's love. Nothing we
can do can make God stop loving us. As George Buttrick once
said, "He never wounds, he eternally woos."

But you ask, "How about His judgments? Isn't God also a
God of justice?" Yes, He is. God has given us the power of
choice. He has, however, set limits; we are not free to choose
the consequences. What we sow, we must reap. This is true for
individuals as it is for groups and nations. But this springs not
from His anger but from His infinite love.

## HIS LOVE AND SUFFERING

The question of suffering is one of the most baffling ever
faced by men. But it is equally as difficult to explain good as
it is to explain evil. For several years there is a drought that
sears the land; fields that once grew from green to gold with
fruitful harvest, now lie parched and barren. "What kind of
God is it that sends us such a plague?" we ask. But did anyone
during all the years of bountiful harvest cry, "O God, the
goodness of Thy bounty and the mystery of Thy generosity is
past our finding out"? Why is it that we think beauty and
blessing are normal to life, while its disappointments and
tragedies are regarded as ruthless intruders? In the same world,
there is the ageless wickedness of war and the unfailing love of
mothers.

On the decks of sinking ships there are men who cry,
"Women and children first," and go bravely to their ocean
tombs. If there is selfishness in the world, there is also the full
giving of love. If we say, "We will no longer struggle with the
problem of suffering; rather we will give up our belief in God,"
then we're left to account for the goodness and heroism of
men, their bright dreams and noble sacrifices, as well as their
genius.

In considering the problem of suffering, we must keep in
mind God's nature. We say glibly, "God is all powerful; why
doesn't He do something? Either He can't stop war, in which

case He is impotent, or else He won't stop war, which means He is not good." But let us look at this concept of omnipotence and find its meaning as applied to Him we call Father.

When God made man in His own image and supplied him with the sublime gift of freedom, He limited Himself. Ever after, there would be things He could not do. That wonderful and awful power of choice which makes man unique is a gift from God, by which He imposes restrictions upon Himself. It is only Omnipotence that can grant such a gift. The very limitation God puts upon Himself is evidence of His power, not of His weakness. Think of this matter of stopping war. It is man who makes war, and every war is against God. Every war is Calvary for God. Every bomb that is exploded opens the wounds of Christ. War goes on because God gave man his freedom—God sought a being who, by his own choice, would love Him and then do justly and love mercy. But no one can choose goodness who has not the power to choose evil. No nation can elect to live as brothers which does not have the power to live like demons.

Why did God not make us otherwise? Why did He not create automatons that cannot do evil and must obey? If He had, the concepts of good and evil would be impossible. If God took away man's power to make choices, He would rob him of his humanity.

God is also limited by the regularity of nature. When God made a world of law, He surrendered His power. We do not mean that God could not intervene and that He had not done so, but when this has occurred it has been through the power of higher laws. We have an orderly world; therefore, it is inevitable that on occasion the regularity of nature will defeat and destroy man. That's what happens when a child slips on ice or falls over a parapet, or when a helpless pilot feels his plane hurtling to earth. Of course, if it were not for this same regularity of nature, no child would ever achieve man's estate nor any plane ever fly the skies.

## *A LOOK AT THE MEANING OF LOVE IN HUMAN RELATIONS*

Love is the truest expression of the self to another person. Fundamentally, love is understanding another. If we have taken the roads to Damascus and Jericho, we understand others and, in a sense, we love all men. In addition, we have no enemies. The person we may consider an enemy is someone we do not understand.

When love is fully expressed, when it is whole, it includes the great meanings that we find in the 13th chapter of First Corinthians.

In its fullest expression love becomes tender and gentle. The self that is a child of God flows into another self until they are as one heart, mind, and soul. The real selves, the Christ-selves become one; they are one in Christ. In this union born of love they see each other as they are and as they can become. The image of what each can be is so clear that the requirements are met for the fulfillment.

This experience of love can be known not only between two, but among a number of people. When a group knows the union of love, Heaven becomes a present reality; the Kingdom has arrived; the group is a microcosm of the Kingdom of Heaven, which is a possibility for all men.

The wholeness of love is realized in the relationships of friendship and marriage. In friendship, the union involves mind and spirit. In marriage, there is a third factor—the union of body. Persons joined in married love are one in mind, heart, and spirit; and their bodies, made with the capacity to desire, seek the union that is already known in spirit. Thus they love each other after the spirit and after the flesh.

Married love should not be the individual's only goal insofar as growth through love is concerned. The whole-making touch of love can be known in friendship with countless persons. Persons who know married love are especially equipped to enlarge the scope of their love. And in doing this, they become agents

in leading others toward wholeness. Healing and wholeness
are only possible through love. Persons who have grown in this
expansive experience of love are not only enroute to Emmaus;
they are taking many along with them. Herein lies the hope
of the world.

## IF ONE CAN'T REACH DAMASCUS

We must tarry here for a while. Many are not free to go to
Jericho, let alone to Emmaus. When one gets to Jericho, he
can reach another person and act with compassion. But the
two persons may or may not feel close. Love is expressed, but
there may be only a sense of helping and being helped. On
the Emmaus road there is more than compassion; there is a
sense of deep belonging. Here, doing, giving, and receiving
are secondary, for the two are so close in union, they are as
one.

One day I drove across our city to see a brother minister who
was ill with cancer. I went out of compassion. We were not
really close. But we respected each other, and there had been
times when we came to each other's defense.

After we had been together for a while, he said, "I'm surprised you are staying so long. You seem so relaxed, so completely with me. Some people start leaving almost as soon as
they arrive. You don't seem to be in a hurry."

"I've wanted to come for several weeks," I replied. "If I'm
not tiring you, I would like to be with you a while longer."

"You're not tiring me; I feel a growing peace with you. I
never before felt close to you, but today I do."

We listened for an hour to each other's words and attended
likewise to our silences. The longer we were together, the
closer we seemed to become. When I arrived, we were at Jericho; and then we headed toward Emmaus. Finally he said,
"Though we've never been close before, we became real friends
today. I can't remember ever feeling so close to a colleague.
Would you give me the sacraments?"

I asked if he wouldn't prefer to have his bishop do it, but he said, "I scarcely know him. It would give me peace to have the loaf and cup given me in friendship." I did so, prayerfully.

A few days later his spirit left his body. But I had the feeling that I hadn't left him nor he me. This is the glorious fact: if two people ever get to Emmaus together, for them there can be no real separation thereafter.

Do you have an idea how many people yearn to go to Emmaus? I have been with young people who got close to Damascus and Jericho, and who had a good start toward Emmaus. When this happens they find it hard to bring the group fellowship to an end. So often persons say to me, "I never felt close to anyone before in my whole life."

I met with a group of six couples who had been joined in a personal growth group for about a year. They had wanted me to address them, but instead I asked, "What have you found in this group fellowship?" They went from one to another and all but one had the same thing to say, "I never really felt close to another person before I got into this group, and never before was I really able to say how I felt. Here I can be myself. Here I can say what I really feel and know that I will be understood." This is true union in friendship.

## SOME SPECIFIC PROPOSALS:

1. Begin consciously to assume the love of people around you and to assume God's love. Act as though you believe you are loved even if you are at first torn with doubt within.

2. Be still and ponder God's love. Open your heart to His love. Beg Him to teach you to love Him.

3. See Jesus as your leader. Read what He said. Study his life, His crucifixion, His triumph over the grave. I found it very helpful to memorize the Sermon on the Mount.

4. Read the great books; listen to the great music; sing the great hymns.

5. Begin to act the way you want to feel. Recently I worked

with a young professional man who was timid. He found social situations enormously painful to him. He was so anxious that sometimes he would walk back and forth in front of a place before he could bring himself to go in, and when he did he was paralyzed. He couldn't say what he wanted to say. It disturbed him so much that he finally came to feel that he couldn't leave home at all.

I listened through a number of visits as he confided his fears and then advised him to this effect: "I have a suggestion which has worked for others, and there's no reason it can't work for you, too. Begin to act the way you want to feel, and one day you actually will feel this way. In other words, when you come to a place where you're threatened, go in and act as if you actually enjoyed being there. You can even enlist God in your duplicity. You might pray to Him in some such way as this: 'Dear Lord, I'm going to go in here and act as if I actually enjoyed it, when in truth I'd like to be a thousand miles away. I'm a hypocrite—I know this—but I'm acting the way I want to feel, and I pray for your help in finding the resource to feel it!'"

He was dubious at first, but finally agreed to give it a try. Within a year he declared, "You know, I can go into any situation today and feel quite at home."

He couldn't have talked himself into it, but by the power of prayer he came to know the truth of the words, "My grace is sufficient for you," and he found his freedom.

Once a young husband brought his wife to me. The problem was that she was not free to respond to his love-making. It had become so serious that when he drove up to the house, she became tense.

She went to a psychiatrist for a few years, but the more she talked about her problem, the more tense she became.

Finally the husband brought her to me with the announcement: "I'll give her two weeks to become my wife or I want a divorce."

I couldn't help but smile. "You paid somebody $25 an hour

for years to help her become free, and now, in two weeks, you expect me to help her for nothing," I said. "If you'll remove the time limit, I think she can be helped." He agreed.

As she talked to me about her background, it came out that she never had been close to her father or mother. There were no expressions of affection among them. She said that on Christmas morning the members of her family often did not even say "Merry Christmas." She grew up without developing the capacity to express tender feelings. Before she got married, her mother said to her, "Sex is just something you have to put up with." She used to hear her father and mother fight over sex relations at night. She heard her mother's cries and her father's heavy breathing. She said she used to lie in bed shivering with fear.

The first night of her marriage she locked herself in the bathroom and would not come out until five o'clock in the morning. By then her husband was asleep, and she timidly lay on the bed beside him, most of her underclothing still on. Her description of the first months of their life together was very touching.

I gave her advice similar to that I gave the timed young man. "If you want to become free to love," I suggested, "you first must act, for you can only act yourself into this capacity you seek. Tonight, when your husband drives up, go out and meet him; hug him, and say something like, 'Darling, I could hardly wait for you to come home.' "

"But, that would be telling a lie," she protested.

"Well, maybe so," I admitted. "But you want it to be true, so you're going to act it. Then in due time you'll actually come to feel it. Give it a try, anyway. Make him think you really want him."

Later that evening her husband called me. "She's off her rocker," he told me. "When I pulled up in front of the house last night she ran out and started climbing all over me. You wouldn't believe the things she said and the way she carried on. But none of it was real; it was put-on. If she isn't off her rocker, she's close to it."

Again I urged patience, and again the young husband agreed. Within five months this woman had achieved the capacity to feel as well as express love, a freedom which was won through her acting the way she wanted to feel until she came to feel it.

In my work with this young woman I kept in touch with the psychiatrist. He himself felt that his patient needed to begin to live the insight she had come to realize. Many counselors and psychiatrists find that there are times when a person needs to *act* himself or herself into the right way of feeling, rather than merely talking. This was true of her. What the psychiatrist did was valid; in cooperating with him I was able to help her find the freedom that was her true nature.

But to return to our specific proposals:

6. Select one person with whom you can have a creative relationship.

7. Take care of things in the past that have produced guilt, for guilt is a block to love. One cannot really love another as long as he can't accept himself; as long as there are things in his life that will not stand the light of day.

8. Develop the skill of really seeing people. Most of us merely look at people. You actually *see* people only when you view them with insight and compassion. Then you look at them not only with your eyes, but with the understanding that comes from the heart.

A second skill is learning to listen to people. This is highly important. When are you truly listening to people? When you hear what they say; when you hear what they are trying to say; and when you hear what their spirit is saying.

9. Open your eyes as you start toward Emmaus. Begin with those you know best, then move to those you know least. Sometimes it's very helpful to start with a lonely person, one who doesn't know how to love, who is timid and withdrawn. Begin with such a person and then, increasingly, the capacity grows.

10. Develop a plan of meditation. There are two kinds of

meditation. One is directed meditation; the other is free meditation. In the last chapter we will go into this in detail. It might follow steps such as these:

*First,* you learn to be receptive. Everything is available to you that you need for the wholeness of your body and for the wholeness of your self; your task is to be receptive to it. The more you are receptive to God and all that's given in life, the more you can become receptive to people.

*Second,* cultivate a sense of the Presence. Keep opening your heart to it, and in due time God will become real. You'll become aware of a Presence—that is, the guardianship of God pervading the atmosphere around you and manifested in the beauty of His world.

*Third,* see others as they are and as they can be. This will save you from coercing others, because you cannot help him you coerce. You can only help him who is ready. If you get a clear image of what another can be, this is really loving him, and the chances are good that ultimately he can become this person.

*Finally,* be thankful. Focus on what you have and not on what you don't have. This leads to wholesome self-sufficiency and genuine graciousness.

## ARE YOU ON YOUR WAY TO EMMAUS?

Again: this is the third great goal as you move toward your highest destiny. The road is not easy, but it leads to life, joy, power, meaning, and peace. You can't go alone. If you are enroute, there are others traveling with you, because this is the nature of the road. With you there will be the One in Whom we live and move and have our being. To miss Emmaus is to miss living, to miss the point of life itself.

# CHAPTER 16. TO BETHLEHEM—INCARNATION

The fourth road to the highest destiny leads to Bethlehem. When one arrives there, the incarnation becomes a reality to him. God poured His life into Jesus that we might see what man can be like with God fully realized in him.

Christ is God made flesh. Jesus is both God's son and God Himself. Were we true to our heritage as children of God, conceived in His image, we would be truly Christlike. When Christ lives in us, we are whole. Then the incarnation, or God's assumption of human form and nature, is a reality made manifest in us.

The plan of God for man, the ultimate goal of creation, is fulfilled in Jesus Christ. His is the example we seek to emulate. To emulate His life and accept His sacrifice is man's highest destiny.

Not for a century has man's purpose been so blurred, so confused by the conflict between his inner longings and his materialism. His conscious focus is on possessions, political movements and organizations, and other aspects of the temporal scene. Thus his inner life is drab; his soul is shriveled; his life has little meaning. He has lost the path to the secret spring. His emphasis is on the body and its comforts, while his soul goes unattended. Yet the spiritual yearnings are there, if atrophied.

## TO THE DEVELOPMENT OF THE INNER LIFE

Carl Jung seems to agree that it is important that we travel this road and develop the inner life. This is how he describes the human condition: "Whether from an intellectual, moral or aesthetic point of view, the undercurrents of the psychic life of the West are a non-inviting picture. We have built a monumental world about us, and we have slaved for it with unequaled energy. But it is so imposing because we have spent upon the outside all that is imposing in our natures—and what we find when we look within must necessarily be as it is, shabby and insufficient."[1]

If this journey is not made we will continue to overemphasize comfort and luxury for the few, rather than liberation for all. To neglect the road to Bethlehem is to render meaningless the previous journeys. For without the cultivation of the inner life, there will be no growth of human sensitivity and no harnessing of the unlimited resources that are the potential of every individual.

Henri Bergson tells us that there is hope for the future only if the interior life of man is cultivated. He says, "Mankind lies groaning, half crushed beneath the weight of his own progress. Now in the body distended out of all proportion, the soul remains what it is, too small to fill it, too weak to guide it. Hence the gap between the two. Hence the tremendous social, political and international problems which are just so many definitions of this gap, and which provoke so many chaotic and ineffectual efforts to fill it. . . . The body now larger calls for a bigger soul. . . . Machinery will find its true vocation again, it will render services in proportion to its power, only if mankind, which it has bowed still lower to the earth, can succeed through it, in standing erect and looking heavenward."[2]

Arnold Toynbee, writing much later than Bergson, points out the same thing when he reminds us that, "From the beginning of the 17th century to the present time, the great genius of man has gone into technical and scientific discoveries, accompanied by a neglect of the inner life."[3] In other words, he is saying that we use research for discovering power, while we neglect the important challenge of research in man, to discover how man's wisdom can be adequate for the proper exercise of the power which has become his.

There are many of the masters whose lives have blessed me. One is that of Theresa of Avila. Someone asked what it was that helped this master of the spiritual life to realize the needs and demands of her time with such penetration, and the answer is, "Precisely the fact that she let herself be drawn even more deeply into the inner parts of her 'interior castle,' even unto that hidden chamber where He could say to her, 'that it was time she took upon her His affairs as if they were her own, and that He would take her affairs upon Himself.' "⁴

It seems to me that this is where each person must be if he is to travel the road to Bethlehem. He comes to understand that the most important thing in the world is to know God, and knowing Him, become alive in Him, thus becoming a part of every problem that faces our world.

## SOME SIGNS THAT MARK THIS ROAD

A person can travel this road, giving himself fully to the will of God, responding to the image of Christ, and realizing that, as he grows, the image of his goal clarifies. He never achieves it, for the more he grows toward its likeness, the more clearly he sees what is demanded of him. Then he discovers that he has just made a beginning. This is one sign. In other words, he pursues a goal he saw in the beginning, and it becomes clarified and enlarged with each step he takes.

We have already mentioned one of the profound principles of life: if one gets the image clear, some profound spiritual law comes into operation by which he meets the requirements to fulfill it.

Another sign is that the more he is drawn toward, and responds to, the Christ-image, the more unique he becomes. As Paul said, "For me to live is Christ" (Phil. 1:21). He who follows Christ is truly himself, fashioned after no other person. As he makes progress, the aspects of him that are a distortion, an illusion, a caricature of the real self, disappear, so that he is more and more the Christ-self; he is God's and God is in him. His being and doing grows in spontaneity, freshness, creativity, joyousness until the whole universe seems to respond to him and the Holy Spirit works in and through his life.

In this growth in his inner life, he is increasingly open before God and with all persons. He can bear nothing in his life that must be kept secret because it is contrary to the person he professes to be. He increasingly is what he says. He prays with all his heart, "Search me and know me and see if there is any evil way in me and lead me in the path of everlasting life." If he does wrong, he confesses it to God and those who are significant in his life. He lives by this in all areas of his life, for otherwise he will become what he withholds. He will become what he keeps secret and not what he tries to make others feel he is.

Thus, if he is open, he is true to his own nature, loyal to the highest he knows. He will then be free to love fully and to be loved fully. He is his real self, the Christ-self, free to love and worth being loved.

A third sign of the road is that those who travel it may not be spared from trouble; instead, they see it as a necessary companion. Those who make progress never ask to be safe; their chief concern is to remain faithful, and this is the theme of their prayers. It was William Russell Maltly who insisted that Jesus promised those who dared follow Him three things: to be "absurdly happy, entirely fearless and always in trouble."

Was not the Psalmist saying the same thing to us in the words, "Whom have I in Heaven but thee? And there is nothing upon earth that I desire beside thee. My flesh and my heart may fail, but God is the strength of my heart and my portion forever" (Ps. 73:25-26).

Those who make progress on the road move toward the fulfillment of the body and the self. Since they are growing in harmony with life, they cannot be responsible for disharmony, but they become objects of hate to those who feel the call of God but refuse to answer it. Moreover, as they seek to fulfill the will of God for social redemption on all fronts, opposition inevitably comes—often with the fury of hell.

Yet they keep on. They find a dauntless courage because, as

they discovered on the road to Emmaus, they are not alone. One has been there ahead of them and travels with them.

A persistent trait of those who take this road is joy. When all illusion is gone, when the real self comes to a sense of being, the inner state is joy. It is not something one achieves, it is something he knows. Jesus tells us He came that we might have joy and that our joy might be complete. Moreover, He said the joy He gave us no man could take away. Never have I seen one who moved toward Bethlehem who wasn't aglow. All I've known were radiant.

Gandhi felt the agony of the world as few persons do, yet we are told that to be with him was to experience joy. He was, of course, unhappy over the human situation, but God used the unhappiness in his mind to mobilize the joy in his heart, that others might be led toward joy.

A final trait we will mention is total commitment to God. One knows that he belongs to God and that all he has and is and can do, is God's. In this commitment, one is not less human; he is truly human. He is not withdrawn from life. Though he learns the ministry of silence alone and in fellowship, he withdraws, not to escape, but to face life, to clarify his vision, to reset his compass away from all the influences that deflect it. But remember, he has been to Jericho and Emmaus. He is himself, but he is in union with God in every man.

The only way one can truly be himself is to give himself fully to God and His will. Then he is growing in the likeness of the Christ-image—giving not getting, caring not ignoring, being trustworthy and not irresponsible.

It is not easy to achieve this. It comes only through an act of surrender; only through total commitment. And one must continue giving himself and all that he has over and over again. Now and then he will break through, giving himself ever more fully. With it all comes a great peace.

He grows increasingly to want what God wants, to feel as God feels, to love as God loves. As he does, fear is canceled, anxiety departs, and the details of life begin to fit together. The more fully one gives himself in dedication, the more he communicates this dedication to others. The more he trusts God, the more he can be trusted.

But such a man goes further. He dedicates his loves, his family, and his work. His work is his way of helping God finish His world. All work is equally sacred if it is equally dedicated. One day he will ordain lay men and women as we do ministers.

Still he goes further. His financial resources belong to God. He now is God's banker. He no longer simply gives alms to God; he pays an interest rate on God's loan of all he has. Depending on how much he trusts God, he will pay all the way from one per cent upward. In some circumstances, a person may pay as much as thirty per cent.

I found some lines that touched me: "Dear God, I give all to you willingly. But I don't know how to give, I just let you take. The best is to remain quiet. Because though I do not know how to give, you know how to take. . . . Yet I would have wished to be once, just once, magnificently generous to you." [5]

## THE PATH OF PRAYER WHICH LEADS THROUGH GETHSEMANE

Progress on all the roads is made only in and through prayer. But this is especially true of this road. There is no inner life without prayer. Prayer is an inner attention to God; it is opening the whole life *to* Him and then *for* Him. Prayer not only involves concentration, but the marshaling of the soul's resources to know God, to respond to God, to love God, to become alive in God, to grow into the likeness of the Christ-image.

Prayer is the heart of all worship; but what is worship? It is man's response in prayer and praise, in confession and adoration, to God's outflow, to His revealing. Worship is man's response to God as revealed in nature, in the divine in man, in the crises of the soul, in Jesus Christ, and by all those in every age who have been fired with the divine spark. It is the experience of the soul searching for its counterpart. Worship is the cry of thirsty land for rain, the quest of a stream for its ocean source. It is the rapture of a poet enthralled by the beauty of a sunrise, the quiet of a workman pausing to listen to a strain of music, the search of a hungry heart for love. It is the engulfing of individual self in the universal self. It is man's ascent of the altar stairs to God, and his return to so live that others may climb; it is the flow of time into eternity.

Worship is commerce between the soul of man and the soul of his Maker. It is a sending forth of the ships of need and their returning, laden with the strength of the Eternal. It is coming into the presence of something mightier than man, which at once humbles him and makes him long to be stronger.

The purpose of worship is the linking of our finite lives with the Infinite life and love of God. Worship is inherent in the nature of man. To ask why he worships is to ask why he breathes.

No one can get to Damascus, Jericho or Emmaus without prayer. But on these roads, prayer is largely on the first two levels—for the self and for others. But to take the road to Bethlehem involves the third level of prayer which is union with God. It reaches Bethlehem and goes on through Gethsemane.

All through his ministry, Jesus prayed. During his forty days which culminated in the temptations, his praying was largely on the first level. Throughout his ministry among men, he often prayed all night. He did this before he chose his disciples. During his three years, he must have prayed mostly on the first two levels—perhaps mostly on the second level, for in the Lord's Prayer and the one in John 17, he is praying for others. The Lord's prayer for *us* is a first-level prayer.

## BEYOND BETHLEHEM IS GETHSEMANE

He went with his disciples, following the Last Supper in the Upper Room, to the garden. He was sorely troubled. The time was at hand. It was a ponderous moment. Would he turn back? He had said that he who takes hold of the plow and turns back is not fit for the Kingdom. Will he turn back? Suppose he had gone to Nazareth! Suppose he had returned to his carpenter's shop! He would be unknown. There would be no New Testament; no Christmas or Easter; no America as we now know it. Think how different music, art, thought, the concept of life and man would be: It is beyond our comprehension.

He asked three disciples to go with him a little further. You remember those amazing moments on which hinged human destiny. He knelt and prayed. Not for himself; not for others, but to come to union with God: "Not my will, but thine be done."

In his humanness, he came to the three asking why they could not watch with him. You recall their answer. Is it not true that although we can only go forward in fellowship, and that only in the redemptive power of fellowship is each person fulfilled, that in the mighty hours of decision each person is alone? In truth, he is not. For though he may be apart from his fellow men in these moments, he is one with God, if he will but allow God to make Himself known to him.

In shedding His blood for the remission of sins, Jesus knew the agony of all men; He felt within Him the world's pain and the sins of men; He heard the cries of hunger for food and love. He was no longer simply Jesus; He was truly Jesus, the Christ.

When anyone moves to the third level of prayer, there is growth; there is fruit; there are all the requirements for the needs of the body and the soul. So it is clear that progress on this road is made only as one makes it a path of high prayer. We must emulate the example of Jesus in Gethsemane just as we accept His sacrifice on Calvary.

## CONCLUSION

We therefore see that this road to Bethlehem—leading to the incarnation, the indwelling Christ, the life of the Divine fully in the soul—is a culminating road, for it leads to the fulfillment of the inner life.

# CHAPTER 17. TO GOLGOTHA AND BEYOND— LIFE ETERNAL

We come now to the final road, the one that leads to Golgotha and beyond Easter. Is it not clear that if we make progress on the other roads, we can then go on to Calvary and take the road that leads through and beyond the final revelation of Easter?

## SOME PRELIMINARY THOUGHTS

Let us make a few things clear at the outset. We are not saved by the *death* of Christ on Calvary, for He did not die. As He said, "I am the resurrection and the life; he that believeth in me, though he were dead, yet shall he live, and whoever lives and believes in me shall never die" (John 11:25).

Obviously, then, we need a new word. His body died; they drove nails into His hands, but not into His soul. On the cross the time came when His body could no longer serve Him, so His Father gave Him a new body. In this way God gave us the revelation that we do not die. The time comes when the spirit leaves the body, for it cannot serve us longer in this dimension, and so we are given a new body.

It was not His death that saved us; it was His love, symbolized most dramatically in the shedding of His blood. Only love saves, heals, and makes whole.

There has been too much emphasis placed on the death of Christ on the cross in terms of its meaning insofar as our salvation is concerned. The crucifixion in and of itself cannot be said to have saved the disciples. With the sight of it they scattered like sheep; they were paralyzed with fear. Peter, who agreed to be crucified with Him, denied Him three times. They were saved after the revelation of Easter morning. Then they became men of courage. In fact, they never grasped the heart of what He sought to reveal until after the final revelation of the resurrection.

## THE MEANING OF CALVARY

On the meaning of this event, as on many others, I am a searcher. I stand in wonder before the mystery of Calvary. To me there are many meanings.

Everything in the life and ministry of Jesus and God's revelation in and through Him was a prelude to the supreme event of Calvary. Here is the heart of our faith. But the revelation of Easter morning fulfilled it, gave it a profound thrust. Pentecost added another thrust.

Calvary is the profound revelation that God's love is without limit. All the rebellion against God, all the sins of men, all the violations of the laws of life, because of Calvary, can be forgiven. Going to Calvary was the mission of Jesus, to be once and for all the proof that nothing can separate man from God's love and grace.

In His trip to the cross, He bore upon himself the sins of all men. He went to Calvary not only to pay the price involved in being true to God and the way of redeeming love, but He went there, taking all who lived before Him and all who would live after Him along. He went, taking you and me along! He thus is saying to us, God is totally present. "If I ascend to heaven, thou art there! If I make my bed in Sheol, thou art there! If I take the wings of the morning and dwell in the uttermost parts of the sea, even there thy hand shall lead me, and thy right hand shall hold me" (Ps. 139:8-10).

Leading up to Calvary, Jesus was saying, "Thy will be done." Those who opposed Him were saying, *"Me; follow me—crucify him!"* He sought what God wanted; they demanded what they wanted. He traveled the roads to Damascus, Jericho, Emmaus, Bethlehem, and Golgotha.

When anyone takes the road to Bethlehem, he inevitably

goes to Golgotha. To be true to the highest means first the crucifixion of the illusion of the self, but then it leads to crucifixion by others of the real self. To be true to the will of God involves one Calvary after another. But finally, if we have been to Bethlehem, each cross becomes a throne.

Why was Jesus crucified? He threatened the vested interests of those whose devotion was to money and power. But, more significantly, He reminded them of the persons they could have been; He set before them the vision of the real self. They either had to respond or destroy him. They chose the latter.

Through His teaching, His example, and His final passion and resurrection, Jesus revealed Himself to be our Saviour. He taught us the way to grow through confession, repentance and restitution, so that we can move from sin to salvation, from bondage to freedom, from sickness to wholeness. Moreover, He made clear that through love, we can grow naturally into freedom, until we come to the high and holy moment when we feel the call of the Holy Spirit and make a response.

On Calvary we see the infinite love of God, His grace and mercy. Like the brilliance of the morning star, we see the forgiving nature of God. In this supreme event, we see the power of divine purpose—the purpose which can mobilize the dream power of mankind; the purpose which calls to the best from the highest. The price of heeding its message becomes nothing when we ponder the quality of life that results.

But Calvary means something more. It tells us that there need be no ultimate defeat; that true friends of God cannot be discouraged; that the saints cannot be insulted; that the Son of God (and hence we) cannot be destroyed.

## BEYOND CALVARY IS EASTER

Our own Calvaries lead to life eternal, the final vindication of man, even as did Christ's Calvary—for the inevitable aftermath of Calvary was the resurrection. And so we need not fear the experience of that which is erroneously called death, for we have the promise of Easter to sustain us. Even the disciples of Jesus were paralyzed by fear until they had experienced the magnificent revelation of Easter. Then they became men of great power and knew a faith that banished fear.

It has been my observation that when a person comes up to the moment when for him times runs out, although he may have been riddled by fear and anxiety during his life, he is then free to trust. This leads me to feel that as he confronts the face of death from a distance, he is shaken by fear; but when he sees the face of Him who said, "lo, I am with you always" (Matt. 28:20), he then sees that death is not death but birth, and all fear goes. Now he knows peace tempered by a new yearning.

Could this mean that all fear springs from the one basic one: the fear of death? Karl Menninger in *Man Against Himself* has a lot to say about the death wish. There are those who feel that the fear of suffering and pain is more basic than the fear of death.

John Erskine well said, "If you have a fear of death, you have missed the point of life." I would like to say that if you have a faith that reaches beyond the experience we erroneously call death, then you have a faith for life.

Let us add one other thought: to have a faith greater than life, to see death as the third birth, in no way diminishes the meaning of life now. But, you say, there are those who are so interested in the new life that they do nothing in this one. This is and can be true. Actually, such persons do not have a faith in life then or now; they are either vegetables or are denying their own destiny. They are running from life, not facing life.

I believe that the more we understand the life beyond, the more precious life is here, and the more we seek to give witness of the truth now.

As for me, I look forward to the next dimension with great curiosity and eagerness, yet I love life now. I want all the time here I can have. There is so much I want to know, so many experiences I seek, so many things I want the Lord to do through me. In fact, I feel about the next dimension as did Peter Marshall, who said: "When the call comes, I'll not be a minute early nor a minute late."

## FAITH IN LIFE BEYOND IS BASIC TO FAITH NOW

This road that goes beyond Easter leads us to a faith that persists, a faith greater than life, and a faith that becomes knowledge.

Faith in immortality persists despite all the logic of time or men. It is a hope that will not die. Sometimes it rises to the majesty of luminous conviction; sometimes it falls to a flickering spark; but it never dies. Relentless rationalism does not smother it, because it hides itself in the heart of the rationalist; cynical despair cannot kill it, for in the night the cynic sees a far, faint star and "listening love hears the rustle of a wing." Whether we doubt or affirm, whether we tread the valleys of doubt or climb the sunlit hills of faith, life keeps burning before our wandering or watchful vision this kindly light of hope. In the heart of every man is a voiceless question—if a man dies, shall he live again? In the heart of everyone is an answer—sometimes the feeble whisper of a forgotten faith, sometimes the song of the soul's assurance—"this is not the end; man was not made to be lost in the deep abyss of nothingness."

Victor Hugo, in words that will be eternal, said, "I feel in myself the future life. I am like a forest cut down; the new shoots are stronger and livelier than ever. I am rising, I know, toward the sky. The sunshine is on my head. The earth gives me its generous sap, but heaven lights me with the reflection of unknown worlds. For half a century I have written my thoughts in prose and in verse; history, philosophy, drama, romance, tradition, satire, ode and song; I've tried all. But I feel I have not said the thousandth part of what is in me. When I go down to the grave I can say like many others, 'I've finished my day's work.' Life is a thoroughfare. It closes on the twilight, it opens on the dawn."[1]

## THE UNIVERSE CONSERVES ALL ENERGY

Energies may be transmuted from form to form—light becomes heat, heat becomes motion—but in all these changes of form there's no annihilation. Today scientists tell us that what we call matter is made up of whirling centers of energy; nothing is static; all is bewildering motion. Will a universe that so carefully husbands all its lesser energies destroy man with his power to think and love and will? When the evolutionary process reaches its apex, does it suddenly reverse itself and begin to destroy energy?

This doesn't make sense. And so this is one of the markers along the road that leads beyond Easter.

## MAN'S NEEDS AND ASPIRATIONS

But there is another. Not only in the nature of man, but in his needs and aspirations, we find strength for this faith. Man's highest human experience is love. The divine in man is that which loves faithfully and purely. When lives have been intertwined in a sacrament of lifelong affection, love does not grow feeble and frail as the years go by. No, as essential threads are interwoven, love becomes an understanding comradeship too deep for words. "These twain are one flesh"—and whenever love kisses the lips of this experience which we erroneously call death, the heart rises in protest, "This cannot be the end, or at least it ought not be the end." There is something too priceless to be lost in the "wide tombs of uncreated night." As Hugh Walpole puts it, "There is a kind of sniff of immortality in their love for one another." In one of Cowper's letters to a friend, the poet said, "There is not time for friendship to unfold itself in such a nook of time as this." No true, loyal love was ever fulfilled in this nook of life.

It is not egotism that leads our souls to demand immortality; it is the most selfless affirmation we can make. One may feel that his survival does not matter, but if these souls whose beauty we have beheld with love's quickening insights are destroyed, then ruling the universe must be wild, archaic forces rejoicing in the destruction of their highest values. Love, with its hunger, its loneliness, its insatiable longing is a prime force of the universe. We have no right to interpret life and leave this fact out of reckoning. What is this experience of life and whence does it come—this cry against the stupidity of annihilation of those whom it adores? A long time ago one who knew love and its meaning said these words: "Faith, hope, and love abide, these three; but the greatest of these is love." Before he uttered this, he said, "Love bears all things, believes all things, hopes all things, endures all things. Love never ends" (1 Cor. 13:7-13).

It seems to come down to this: if death is the end, then the person we love is dust, or electrical energy arranged in patterns. It's just impossible for us to believe that a person we love is dust. Who in the world could believe that Jesus Christ is dust?

## WHEN LIFE IS UNFULFILLED

When the long evening is drawing on, the philosopher lays down his pen and says, "I have just begun"; the artist yields up his brush knowing that his masterpiece is a faint symbol of the beauty his soul has seen; the saint is well aware that he has not learned the alphabet of godliness. In every soul, there are withheld completions, masses of beginnings without endings, foundations laid for temples unbuilt, ships lost that shall never sail the sea. It is this intuitive belief that their aspirations have meaning in the universe that keeps men struggling upward in what seems an alien world.

I often think of the story of the little boy who in the late afternoon was building a city from sand on the seashore. For a long time he toiled, so engrossed in his work that he did not notice the hour was getting late and that the tide was coming in. Then one wave, mightier than the rest, swept in, washing away his houses and streets, his city and outlying farms. In terror, the child ran back to the cliffs. But on the bank above his older brother had been watching him. He was thinking how he too once played on the seashore. He reached down and helped his younger brother up the bank, comforting him in his distress. Through the gathering gloom they walked toward the gleaming lights of home where awaited rest and refreshment, further discipline and high achievement. So at last, He who called Himself a brother will lead us beyond the sands of time and place, to our Father's house—to undertake other tasks for which life has been both discipline and preparation.

Life is a mass of beginnings without end. There is so much here that is yet unfinished. There must be for the musician, for example, a greater keyboard where the improvisations for which he can find no expression can be fully realized.

## THE TESTIMONY OF THOSE IN THE ULTIMATE MOMENT

There is one other sign along the road: Those who come up to the final moment say there's something that lies beyond. This was true of the disciples as they approached the ultimate moment. And I have witnessed it again and again as I have attended people in their last hours.

Once I ministered to a young woman of twenty-eight whose body could no longer serve her. One night I felt compelled to go to her home, and as I entered, her young husband said: "I've been trying to reach you all evening. I'm so glad you came."

I went into the room where she lay. She asked me to anoint her body and administer the sacraments. Then she said, "Tell me what it will be like."

"God will speak to you," I told her. "He will explain that your body cannot serve you any longer, and He will give you a new body. When you rise up as you have many times before, it will be with a new freedom and strength and joy. And from thenceforth you will be with your husband, your children, your parents—with all your loved ones—and with your Heavenly Father all at the same time."

She smiled and said, "I've heard you say something like that many times before, but now I know it's true."

In due time I left. The next morning at five o'clock I was suddenly awakened. I thought I heard the telephone ring, but I was mistaken. Later I received a message to call the husband. When he answered I asked, "Was it at five o'clock that it happened?"

He said, "Yes, but who told you?"

"Marilyn," I said.

## CONCLUSION

The road to Golgotha is the ultimate road. It goes to Easter and reaches beyond. In traveling it, we can experience the Kingdom of Heaven in this life, and in such a way as to prepare us for the actual living Presence in the Hereafter.

# PART IV. WHOLE-MAKING RELATIONS

## CHAPTER 18. THE CHURCH

It is in whole-making relationships that people can make not only a beginning and tap the unfailing resources, but travel the roads that lead to their highest destiny.

The church is a laboratory center.

### THE CHURCH AND ITS NATURE

On hills and in valleys, in hamlets and towns, in urban centers and great cities, there are buildings that have been dedicated to worship. Rising from many of them are steeples pointing heavenward, and over scores of them are crosses marking the skyline. Most of them are simple, rectangular buildings with one room; others have a sanctuary with additional rooms for study and social activities; and a few are exquisite Gothic structures that cost millions of dollars to build.

We call them churches, but they are not The Church. They are made of stone, brick, mortar, and wood. They are sacred places rather than consecrated relationships. They stand on hallowed ground, but they are not spiritual. They are temporal, not eternal. The church is spiritual when in it Heaven and earth meet; when through it the highlands of God join the lowlands of men.

The church is a fellowship of those who are trying to find

out who they are, those who are joined in a relationship in which they call to the best in each other and mobilize the finest in each.

The church has been in the world since man became aware, for where two or more have gathered together to search out the secret of life, to discover the highest and best, to come to know the meaning of life, there was the church. It has taken many forms and used many names. Sometimes this fellowship uses strong buildings, fine places, expensive settings. Oftentimes the fellowship is known in homes and in simple places.

In varying degrees, the church has kept alive the spirit of compassion through the years. At its best it has provided an enlightened conscience, and has been the custodian of the glorious Gospel. Always there has been a remnant, a few like those who belong to the company of Anna, of whom it was said that she waited for the redemption of Israel. The followers of Jesus in the early church had a power that the later church lost and has never fully recovered since Augustine, even in the most spiritually vivid years of its history. But always there has been a remnant—those few who waited for the morning, who joined together from the high places and the low, who kept the flame of their faith burning in the altars of their hearts.

Amid the spiritual sterility and lethargy of their times, they were divinely discontent, wistful, devout, expectant. There were the supremely dedicated Puritans of England, the persecuted Presbyterians of the Scottish Highlands, the Waldensians of the Italian mountains, the members of the Dutch Church during the last war, who drew together secretely in barns or cottage kitchens or woodland glens to spend some hours in prayer and study of the Word. In all ages they have lived—those who scanned the stormy horizon watching for the dawn, who, in the darkest night, confidently expected the daybreak. What a debt civilization owes them!

## THE CONTEMPORARY CHURCH

Before we elaborate further on how the church can foster whole-making relationships, let us look for a moment at the contemporary church. I feel that there is an awakening, a growing awareness that is leading to a new church—what we might call the "true church." Sometimes I find it in simple places like a prayer center in Tucson or Cincinnati or a house like Shadybrook in Cleveland. Sometimes I find it in small rural churches, sometimes in downtown churches, though not as often.

Never have I sensed such interest on the part of laymen in discovering the true meaning of the church and what it stands for. Never have I seen ministers so eager to learn, to understand how the church can foster whole-making relationships; how it can become a whole-making fellowship. There is a new church developing. There is a new spirit growing. And yet the modern church has shortcomings that we should face.

1. Despite the threat of nuclear suicide, the local church is strangely silent. In the face of the agony in underdeveloped areas; the untold suffering among the world's refugees; the hungry, sick, and needy children of the world—the response of local church members, though there is evidence of interest, is meager in light of the potential.

Giving to World Missions is less than two dollars per person per year. While there is great work being done by agencies like our mission boards and Church World Service, if church members really cared, this useful work could grow in power until it made a great impact. It is exciting to imagine what could happen if those who are part of a living church would really respond.

2. It is my impression that a large majority of people join the church as a substitute for Christian living. Only about one-third of the members of a church are active. Some recent studies have indicated that a year after persons join, one-third are already inactive. With the exception of Jehovah's Witnesses, Christian Scientists, Seventh-Day Adventists, and the Mormons, the dif-

ference between those who belong to the church and those who don't is not very discernible.

The contemporary church is made up of millions of people who, like Joseph of Arimathea, are secret disciples with half-hearted loyalty. These persons want the Kingdom of God but do not want it first; the love of God is second to love of power, money, security, and pleasure. The contemporary church in large majority is composed of persons who hold in their hearts a deep conviction that there is something greater in life than they are, something they call God. They contemplate with horror a world that would rob them of the freedom of worship, and yet they do not give their wholehearted loyalty to God. They try to walk in the ways of the Master; they want His approval; in times of disappointment and sorrow they lean upon the great assurances that are to be found in religion. In their hearts they believe in the God of love and mercy. But never do they fully and enthusiastically declare, "I'm on His side; I acknowledge my debt to Him and I will do my share in making His spirit and His purpose prevail in human society."

If all the half-loyalty and the secret discipleship and the lukewarm fealty that are accorded to God were suddenly to flame into fiery, zealous devotion, this generation would save an imperiled civilization. There is less and less room today for secret and divided loyalties. A communist will sacrifice to uphold the preachments of the communist creed and will boast his faith on the street corner. Every anti-Christian dogma demands of its followers wholehearted, singleminded devotion, a loyalty bravely and sincerely proclaimed. Least of all times in history can we afford a religious faith that is vague and undefined, a surreptitious lip service, a shrewd mixture of idealism and worldly astuteness that cautiously seeks to gain Heaven without losing hold of earth.

In fact, there is a mass movement into the front door of the church while a large percentage go out the back door. Even those who stay and are most active are not certain what religion is all about. I have met key members of churches in retreats all over the country and, in most cases, they are very unclear about their faith, both in theological and in personal terms.

3. The major emphasis in the average church is on the hour of worship. Thus the focus is on adults. The money is spent on this one aspect. Most churches have trained people for preaching, pastoral work, and music. Only a few have trained persons working with children and youth. And yet what happens in the nursery and kindergarten may be more important than what happens in the pulpit.

In most churches the emphasis is on what is being done *to* people. The method is talking. In the contemporary church the leaders talk but rarely listen. Little happens to a person while he listens; much can happen while he is being listened to. If he is listened to with understanding, he may then be able to hear. We will elaborate further on this later. Churches that only do things *to* people are not real; the true church involves a fellowship in which the right things happen in and through individuals.

4. Because of a lack of real spiritual nurture in the contemporary church, there are a number of observations I am led to make. First, in many local churches there are cold wars and civil wars among the members and among church staffs. This is an indication that they come into the church seeking help, and when they do not find it, they give expression in negative terms.

There is a growth of movements that seek to provide experiences in depth. Some are highly constructive, while others get persons off focus. For some, these actually become a substitute for the local church. For others, they become the real church. When they go back to their churches out of a sense of obligation, they become frustrated by their lack of meaning.

On campuses, in professional groups, and in other enterprises, there is a growth of small groups which are more truly the church than is the church. The summer conferences for youth usually become vital spiritual fellowships, but when these young people return to the home church, often they find no support and so go back to conforming to secular stereotypes.

5. The local church "plays safe" on such issues as racial integration by remaining silent. With the growth of the hate groups, the church leaders may become more and more harmless. The situation is so serious in some communities that people are afraid to let their neighbors see the pastor call. In such conditions the church could lose its redemptive power, and thus be shaped by the neighborhood rather than be a redeeming force in it.

6. Often local churches become competitive, especially in the smaller communities. This is a serious situation. In many of these communities there are outstanding high schools, for example. Here young people have the best facilities. In some of them there are outstanding acappella choirs; they have assemblies that are an inspiration, where all of the resources for great experiences are made available. By contrast, the churches are little, one-room buildings, often unattractive, some of them served by a part-time minister. In one state, I understand there are 2,000 churches without ministers, being too small to support a pastor. Now and then I meet a minister who is asked to give leadership to as many as eight local churches.

The competitive situation among churches is spiritually damaging in larger communities. In each, the God of love is taught and preached but by the attitudes among the churches, He is denied. Churches, instead of co-operating with one another, often seek to outdo each other.

There are many injurious results. Children go to the same school, but on Sunday morning they are separated. Young people cheer for the same team but become divided before the altar of God. Adults join in all other activities, but in their spiritual life they become separated by labels and institutional loyalties.

The ideal would be one church for each elementary school district. The church membership should be made up of a neighborhood. Then there would be resources to provide the leadership and equipment needed. Then the church could preach love, and the word *community* would acquire real meaning; then the ministry could achieve a quality of excellence and maturity. And then the church, in the deepest sense, could become a whole-making fellowship.

## A NEW CHURCH IS COMING TO BE

While the foregoing views of the contemporary church are valid, I want to go further to say that a new church is coming to be. Its growth is gradual, but it is real. These are the signs:

1. Ministers are learning how to counsel, to help troubled people, to build a fellowship in which individuals can grow.

2. There is the development of small groups such as we have discussed and will discuss further in Chapter 21. Essentially these groups are concerned with prayer or spiritual research. These are growing up in all parts of the country, and, where they are really developed, new life has come into the church.

3. While some services of worship are becoming more formal, in many places there are growing a variety of expressions of religious experience. For example, there is increased participation in worship. In one service there may be one, two, or a half dozen laymen other than the choir who participate in the leadership. In several churches there is the regular service with a sermon, followed by responses from the people. Some churches use dialogues, role-playing or dramatic worship settings to help people see the truth of the message. Some use visual aids of various kinds, knowing that people see better than they hear.

4. There are a growing number of week-end retreats, conferences, and special seminars. Such groups as Camps Farthest Out, Prayer Life Movement, Yokefellow Movement, and the Disciplined Order are making great impact.

5. Constructive religious radio and television programs are of great value. There are a growing number of worthwhile books in the field of prayer and the life of the spirit.

6. In business and professional groups, there is often a very

fine spiritual quality achieved in efforts to enrich the lives of their memberships.

## WHEN THE FELLOWSHIP LEADS TO WHOLENESS

There is not space to spell out in detail the way in which the church can foster whole-making relationships. We can only briefly describe the main aspects.

1. Ministry extends from conception across all the seasons of life.

*Prenatal.* In Chapter II we described how the requirements can be met for a baby to be conceived and born in love. Since the purpose of the church is to become the fellowship in which three healthy births take place—into the body, into the spirit and into the next dimension—we want to do everything to make the first birth as conducive to health and wholeness as we can.

*The second birth.* From the moment of conception, everything that becomes a part of the experience of the person prepares him for the process of the second birth. Jesus said, "You must be born anew" (John 3:7). The five roads we have traveled provide the beginning of the ongoing development in this birth into the spirit, so that the person coming to be shall be the one God intends.

*Preschool.* When the baby is born, he immediately becomes a part of the church fellowship. First there is baptism. His religious education insofar as the church is concerned begins in the toddler years, when he joins the Sunday School program in the Nursery—from which he "graduates" to the Kindergarten. Many churches have day nurseries and kindergartens if such are not provided by the public schools.

*The fist six grades.* The Sunday School program during these years becomes combined with some experiences provided in the Sunday program, and through the week there may be programs for released time from school or special sessions on Saturday. At the end of the sixth grade, there should be some symbol to mark the stage of growth, perhaps a little copy of the Golden Rule. This kind of a symbol would be very appropriate, for boys and girls at this age are beginning to develop responsible interpersonal relationships and the symbol of the Golden Rule would have real meaning.

Through these years teachers should be sensitive to the children, sensing when there is stress in the home relationships. Contacts can then be made with the parents. Thus far-reaching preventative work can be done.

*Junior high.* We did not develop in detail the work with small children, but because of the strategic importance of junior high and senior high young people, we will give a little more attention to them. In the seventh and eighth grades the emphasis is on moving from childhood into the official church family. Two years are spent on this emphasis.

In many churches boys and girls are confirmed as church members at the end of the sixth grade. This is a mistake, for they are then not yet in puberty when they are taken into the adult fellowship. This is too early for them, both socially and intellectually. At the end of the eighth grade most of them are through puberty; the gift of manhood has been given to the boys and the gift of womanhood has come to girls. They now have the feeling of the male and the female. If they were in India they might marry and begin their families.

During these two years of preparation, the emphasis in our fellowship is upon understanding and appreciating the physical body and coming to know the outstanding characters of the Bible and of human history. This is offered in the first person. That is, someone actually takes the role of the historical person. This is very meaningful because truth is most telling when it is given the trappings of personality. There is study, especially of Jesus and His meaning in life, of the appreciation of worship and the meaning of prayer, and of the development of leadership skills. There is consideration of the community and a greater appreciation of the world and the world's peoples; there is a study of friendship and dating.

The church directs the young people toward a growing appreciation of the meaning of the self and the possibilities of the individual. Throughout these years, the young people are led to know the spirit and life of Jesus Christ, to know what it means to follow Him, make a commitment to Him and His way, and then, finally, to become a vital part of the body of those who are seeking to move into the wholeness of the person.

At the end of the eighth grade, they are no longer children. They now have the capacity to create life. They are actually young adults, and so they enter into the full life of the church. At this time they receive a block of wood with the understanding that they will never tell its meaning in spoken or written word, but so live that others in due time will know the meaning.

This block of wood relates to an old legend. When Jesus was crucified, someone asked where they got the wood for the cross. A woodsman discovered the stump of the tree, and it became a sacred place. In time a new shoot was discovered growing up from the old root. And it was said, "The spirit of Jesus lives on as does the tree." A decision was made to cut down the tree and make the wood into crosses to be distributed to the churches, for this was a time when Christians were under great stress. The wood that could not be made into crosses was made into little blocks and given, in the manner described above, to young Christians. The idea was that it is so easy to speak words but far more difficult to practice what is spoken. It is reported that those who wear the block of wood on their person are protected and will have a special resource of courage.

*Senior high.* In the years beyond the eighth grade, we deal with the four years of senior high school. It is true that in many school districts the ninth grade, along with the seventh and eighth, is a part of the senior high system. There are many reasons for this. However, there is a very great difference between a ninth grader and a seventh grader. In our fellowship we prefer to work with the four grades together, and, while the symbol for the eighth grade graduate is a block of wood, the ninth grade is the Reminder of the 7 Keys, and the graduates (or their equivalents in age) of the senior high school can win certificates of leadership.

The emphasis in the ninth grade is on coming to know the self—this new self, this true self, this self that they must love if they are to love others and God.

The emphasis in the tenth grade is on knowing the other person; it is on the love in friendship between girl and girl, boy and boy, boy and girl, parent and child, and child and parent. There is a carefully planned approach that will help the individual boys and girls to know how to become a part of a group and still be individuals. There is an effort to help them come to an appreciation of the family and all of the institutions that are so significant in the free world.

In the junior year, or eleventh grade, there is an effort to help young people find the theology of human relations, a faith to live by, and the application of this faith in friendship, in married love, in work, and in living with all persons irrespective of color, race, or creed. They are alerted to the challenge to live their religion and to work on the unsolved problems of the community and the world.

In the twelfth grade there is a focusing on vocational choice, on citizenship, on the developing of dynamic skills of leadership, and on understanding the world in which they live and the world task that is before them.

Through all the four years the individuals are asked to meet various requirements—for example: participation in camps and in research in prayer; leadership in various departments of the church, and in the school and community; development of various leadership skills; the perfecting of a philosophy of life and especially a living faith; gaining a knowledge of the Bible, and of the great religious sources of the church and of the world.

If these requirements have been met, when these young people come to the end of their high school years, they receive certificates of leadership in a public service. This certificate has such value that it has been recognized by some colleges and future employers. When he sees the requirements that had to be met to win this certificate, the school authority or the employer recognizes its significance.[2]

*Beyond high school.* The years from eighteen to twenty-one are very important. If the young person goes to college, he can soon get so involved in the campus life that he may withdraw from the church and thus neglect the spiritual development of his life. This happens often and is a serious loss.

If they go to work or marry young, persons of this age often drift away, become engrossed with vocational, family and social demands, and neglect the most important aspect of life, the ongoing experience of their spiritual development.

Each local church must meet this challenge in its own way. On campuses there are student programs of various denominations. But these care for only those who participate. More effective work could be done if leaders met regularly with student groups, thus carrying the ministry to the students.

In the parish where I worked for a number of years, our work with the college age included these features: a Sunday evening session at five o'clock, a Wednesday night spiritual research session at six o'clock, a camp held over Labor Day week-end, a New Year's Eve retreat with a midnight communion service, and another retreat during the spring vacation. Then there is a plan whereby ministers and laymen go to dormitories, fraternities, sororities, and meet with other campus groups. Often after one of these evenings the whole group would attend church the following Sunday.

In this parish there is a group called The Keys whose purpose is to win and share with others the keys to the Kingdom, for the only way they can be kept is for them to be given away.

We will be thinking of these "keys" in the final chapter when we see how each person can evaluate his growth.

*Beyond college age.* It is not enough for the church to have a cumulative program through the college age. If, beyond this age, persons remain unmarried, there must be a place for them. In our spiritual laboratory there is a Cambridge Club for persons between the age of twenty-one and forty. There are a number of marriages each year in this group. We are always looking for young men for this club. When they are enlisted, the women do the rest.

If they are not married at forty, they go into the Community Club, which is for unmarried people from forty to fifty. If they are single at fifty, they enter the Over-Fifty Club and stay there as long as they live in the body.

When persons are married they join the Couples' Club. When they are expecting their first child, they can become a part of workshops, personal growth groups, and other special research groups which will be described in Chapter 21.

After retirement, couples may join the Century Club which provides rich experiences in study, fellowship, and spiritual inspiration. Women sixty-five and older can become a part of the Sweethearts' Club, in which they receive special ministry and become a part of the intercessory prayer groups.

*Group worship.* Actually, of course, the heart of the church experience is in the sanctuary, but the vitality of this experience depends on what is going on in the various small groups. If the church provides real nurture from conception through all the years of life, the person comes to insights and understandings and appreciations which make it possible for him to join with others in meaningful and profound worship. I am not going into this in great detail, for I am preparing a book directed to young ministers in which I will elaborate on the place and function of worship.

Suffice it to say that worship is the act by which individuals join together in an experience of God. It is the heart of life. Prayer is the master key and the heart of worship.

Previously we have discussed the various manifestations of the hour of worship, stressing experiments which help people see more clearly, which provide increased participation, and which attempt to make clear the truth of which the church is a witness.

Perhaps equally as important as the hour of worship are the worship experiences that grow up informally. A group may be on a retreat over a week-end; they may have an experience of spiritual communion which becomes unusually meaningful. At the close of the meeting of a small youth group, those present may stand in a circle with clasped hands and pray individually. Such experiences are vital. Oftentimes special worship settings are prepared to bring people to the moment of prayer. The creative use of such symbols as color, lighting, the spoken voice, or music add to the whole experience and bring truth in a vivid form to people.

So in any spiritual laboratory it is important that all gather together in an inspiring experience of worship, but they should also have these experiences in small groups in which they come to a sense of God and the Eternal Presence.

2. The work of the church focuses on marriage and the family. In Chapter 19 we will deal in more detail with the family to see how it can provide whole-making relationships. One of the fundamental purposes of the spiritual laboratory is to help the family become whole, that it may be the source of healthy relationships. For if the church is the body of Christ, the family is the cell.

3. There is a plan of therapy and healing. In the church the most important counseling is initiated for positive prevention. In our laboratory, for example, we had all young people in the ninth grade fill out a personality inventory. We said we would help them draw a picture of their behavior. Then I would see them individually on Saturday morning. If deviations from the normal were indicated, we could guide them in a retraining experience. In cases of extreme mood swings or marked regressive behavior, we sought the co-operation of a physician. The results of this were far-reaching. It is perhaps one reason that we had 646 men and boys in the last war without one emotional breakdown; not one discharge for psychoneurotic reasons.

In the eleventh grade we ran a vocational test. Twelfth

graders made the same inventory previously done in the ninth grade. Then I saw only those whose picture indicated a need.

We saw all persons before they left for college, and kept in touch with them, and all who were taking jobs. In the case of many, we worked with them before they went to the first job.

We made use of group therapy. There were regular workshops for parents of preschool and elementary school children, for youth, for husbands and wives, and for expectant parents.

For years we held group interviews, a series of five in the fall, another in the winter, and a third in the spring. These dealt with very specific questions, such as how to put children to bed or how to deal with a silent husband or a talkative wife.

4. There can be a very meaningful reciprocal ministry. In a growing spiritual laboratory there may be one or more ministers who are specially trained to give particular attention to pastoral work. But one of the major tasks is always to discover and train laymen. Groups of men and women can be trained, for example, to maintain contact with certain families. This can be a regular part of the work, and with most families it can reap great benefits.

There are, in addition, a growing number of people who can become the "significant person" in the life of one in need. A widow or widower who survived grief can work with one who is going through this experience; couples who come to deeper union can work with a couple in need. For example, a couple may not find fulfillment in their sexual life, or they may have difficulty in handling a budget, or they may overreact to certain situations. Often another couple with insight can be helpful. A couple who are overanxious about toilet training may be helped by another who have come to greater understanding along this line. Parents, finding understanding in their own spiritual life, can be helpful to other parents. Or a couple, having come to grips with the problem of setting limits with their children, may help other parents with this problem.

It can go further than this, as it did in the laboratory where I worked for many years. A woman is rejected, for example. One night her husband comes home and says, "I'm through. I love somebody else." Another woman is asked to work with her—stick with her until the problem is solved. Maybe a professional staff member will work with the husband.

Another person may be asked to establish contact with a woman in a mental hospital, so that when she is discharged she will have a friend to help her find meaningful relationships. No one can estimate the far-reaching help that can be rendered to such a person who has the task of rebuilding her life.

The object should always be to help people grow into wholeness from conception; and, if they become blocked along the way, to help them become free. In no laboratory is the job ever fully done, but I have been struck by the number of people I have seen become part of the team to help others move from where they were toward their highest destiny.

5. There is a ministry that reaches beyond the laboratory, beyond the walls of the church.

It is very important that church leaders work closely with the school. The more adults in a child's life there are who relate to him in an intelligent, imaginative way, the more he will be helped toward freedom of the self and ultimate responsibility. Let me give you an example of the sort of co-operation that I would like to see become widespread. A boy in the fourth grade of one of our city's schools withdrew into a world of fantasy to such an extent that his teacher became concerned and reported to the principal. The principal in turn contacted a member of our staff. Although the family were not of our church, someone made a call on them.

As is usually the case, the boy's problems could be traced to family stresses. However, the parents proved amenable to counseling, and finally they even became members of our church. As the home, church, and school pooled their resources, the boy began to develop normally.

Or consider the high school girl who imagined she was a movie star. "But that's normal for a young girl," you may protest. And you could be right. But this girl went farther than most. It was a girl-friend who had played with her from earliest childhood whose concern directed her to me. Ellen was an active member of our youth fellowship. "You see, Sally doesn't date, and she didn't get into a sorority," she explained. "She tries so hard to get into a school play, and she's always turned down. She gets her only satisfaction imagining she's someone else. Do you think you could talk Mr. Mosing into giving her a chance in a play?"

I went to see Mr. Mosing, the school's drama director, and was able to persuade him to give the girl a small part in one of his productions. The reason he gave for turning her down previously was her lack of talent. He said that if she did have any ability, her affectations kept it hidden and alienated the other students. This, he said, would make it difficult for him to get the measure of co-operation he would need to put on a successful show. Nevertheless, he did agree to try her in a small role. This proved to be a beginning for the girl. Accepted to this degree, she began to shed her mannerisms and her pose. She performed really very well, and I was told that bigger and meatier roles would follow.

Ellen persuaded her to join our youth group in church, too. In due time she even began to date boys in the group. Meanwhile, we arranged behind the scenes for her to get to know one of our older women who had a touch with young people. This woman had also been a drama coach, and she helped Sally with her acting technique as well as in her over-all social adjustment and attitudes. Increasingly, Sally came to know and accept herself. In doing this, she lost the need to be someone else.

Throughout all this, no one dealt with her directly. That is, she was unaware—and still is—that there was a "plot" afoot. I didn't ever have a "heart-to-heart" talk with her. Several of us simply co-operated unobtrusively to reorganize the girl's environment.

So teamwork between the school and the spiritual laboratory has unlimited possibilities.

Such teamwork also needs to be carried on in co-operation

with the community's various social agencies; the police and the courts. Through the years our spiritual laboratory has helped many boys and girls in trouble who were referred to us. Only once in all the years did we have to return a young person to the authorities. This was a girl who was finally placed in a corrective institution for a period. Ultimately, she did acquire self-discipline, and today she's a happily married woman.

The ministry of the church should reach out into the needy areas of the community. One of our efforts along these lines culminated in the formation of a neighborhood council.

But the ministry needs to go further. It must reach out to embrace the suffering mass of mankind. It must discover ways to cope with the great world issues in a dynamic and constructive way. It is not enough for wholeness to grow in the community; the healing force of love and the sharing of knowledge must reach beyond the community, beyond state boundaries, beyond our nation. We must come to grips with the pressing problems of our own society, but we must confront finally the problem of suffering mankind everywhere. Many people are doing the latter by contributing to, or working for, such UN agencies as UNICEF, WHO, and UNESCO; and such private agencies as World Neighbors, Agricultural Aid, Agricultural Missions, and CARE. Much of such effort is conducted through local churches.

Thus people who are finding the way to wholeness individually and locally are discovering ways in which they can join with people in the far reaches of the world to find wholeness. The church is a whole-making fellowship in terms of individuals, the community, and the world.

# CHAPTER 19. THE FAMILY

The family is the primary unit. Despite all the divorces and all the marriages that fall short of the ideal, I believe that today's family promises greater fulfillment than ever before.

Why? Never was so much thought given to the home. There is increasing recognition by every educational medium that knowledge and training are as necessary for marriage and family life as for any skill or profession.

One of the phenomena of our time is the widespread interest of youth in love and marriage. Our magazines regularly include articles on marriage, the family, and love. There are countless books written on the subject. Colleges and universities provide courses. Family guidance centers are found in every population center.

Increasingly the family and marriage are emphasized in medical schools, seminaries, and other professional schools. I was privileged to teach one of the first courses on the physician and marriage ever given in a medical school; now the emphasis is universal. For many years, few ministers stressed premarital training; now almost every responsible church considers this an essential ministry.

The emphasis on child care, mental hygiene, child guidance and parent training is omnipresent. There are mothers' groups, parents' groups, and child guidance groups so numerous that parents get worn out attending them. Parents know more about the child and his care now than ever before. Fathers are better informed and more concerned today and thus give more time to their children. Entire families come into the church today. Not enough happens to them in most cases, but they are there, and they're eager to learn.

And so despite the fact that so many marriages are unhappy,

I believe we are making progress. One thing is sure—two people can gain the freedom to love each other through a lifetime. And they can become free to live with their children in a way that leads to wholeness.

If they get the right start, if they use the unfailing resources of which we spoke, and then take the five roads to destiny of the self, their home will become an example of the kind of world that dreamers have always envisioned.

## THE MALE ROLE

We have pointed out instances of the unfulfillment of fathers and husbands. Now, why should this be so widespread?

Many articles appear in magazines with such titles as, "The Crisis of the American Male," or, interestingly enough, "The Crisis of the American Female." Such articles as the former discuss the confusion of the American male because of his displacement as incontrovertible head of the household. The wife may work, thus removing her husband from his position as sole provider; and, in any case, she shares in the kinds of responsibilities and decisions that formerly defined his domain. In the reshuffling, moreover, he has taken on his share of her responsibilities, with the result that often both husbands and wives are unsure as to who they are. And yet these changes that we see taking place in the respective roles of husband and wife, mother and father, can have salutary results if persons can cease being ruled by stereotypes. Is it not true, for instance, that children need love and tenderness as much as their bodies need oxygen, food, and vitamins? Insofar as the current "crisis" is determined by false conceptions of masculinity, it is a paper crisis. For tenderness should certainly be as much a masculine component as an indication of femininity. Jesus, Gandhi, St. Francis, Albert Schweitzer cannot be deemed less masculine because of their gentleness and compassion.

We have always emphasized mother love at the expense of father love. Yet both are equally important. I view with heartfelt approval the modern trend to give the father his due. If confusion results as roles are re-evaluated and in the process of definition, this is a small price to pay for the promised return on investment. Colonel Farley, founder of Boys' Ranch, has observed that ninety per cent of the youngsters who come to him are products of homes where there was little or no father influence. Similarly, Father Flanagan reports that in the background of almost every boy offender is a story of shocking neglect, and that between eighty and ninety per cent of the boys in Boys Town who have been in trouble came from homes broken by divorce, separation, or death, or from homes where it was impossible to have a real relationship with father and mother. Judge Leibowitz, of Brooklyn's highest criminal court, has concluded that the Number One factor in criminality is unfulfillment of the father role. Thus, if the family is to provide whole-making relationships, the man must be a good husband to help his wife be a good mother, and then, in the fullness of his manhood, accept the loving responsibility of his fatherhood.

## FUNCTIONS OF THE FAMILY

Once the family was the center of a person's whole life. It combined with the functions of school and church, where these were present, and substituted for them where they were absent. The members not only lived together, but shared most of life's experiences. One hundred years ago, eighty per cent of America's families lived in rural areas, with all members tilling the soil and working together. Today this is no longer true. Less than twenty per cent are now rural. Fathers leave home to go to work; twelve million wives work outside the home. Other institutions have taken over many of the functions—such as education and religious training—that once belonged primarily to the family; and most leisure time is spent outside the home. There are a host of groups taking the family away from the home. The unfortunate result is that home often becomes a way station.

What functions remain? One is that which results in two people joining together in a lifetime of mutual love. Only a small percentage realize this in full, but if the observation that the modern family is coming into its own is not overly optimistic, this number will increase. And, as it does, a new world will unfold, populated with persons with the capacity to live creatively within it.

Here and there a new culture of courtship is growing up. Young couples are coming to see the difference between real love and the game of love. They are becoming aware that any two people with a little technique can make love, and that a meaningful relationship is a far greater challenge. They are coming to see that marriage is more than kisses. Girls are realizing that if they give their bodies too soon, *they* will never be wanted. Once I asked a girl who insisted on many dates before she would enter into limited love-making, "Why do you set such a price on your kisses?" Her answer was interesting: "If I give my lips too soon, he will never want *me*."

This does not mean that such girls are frigid. They recognize sexual desire as God-given. They look forward to fulfillment with anticipation. But they also know that to respond because of the desire of the moment is to be a creature of impulse. Though they accept the capacity for desire, to love after the flesh, as God-given, they know that it is important to express the desire in harmony with the wisdom of time.

A growing number of boys are willing to exercise the same restraint. They recognize that if they give the physical the primary emphasis, and if they become one in body before the wedding, the physical will dominate the relationship. They will fail to cultivate the companionship and friendship that is needed to build a meaningful way of life. Then, after the wedding, this in which they have specialized is not enough. They have not won the freedom to know great union; they have gone only a little way on the roads of destiny; they made the prelude the symphony; they have had each other's bodies, but they never really became one. They denied their highest destiny.

Moreover, to focus on the physical sharing causes other problems. It creates either anxiety or pregnancy, or both. Moreover, the male, having found biological fulfillment, often loses interest. And as his interest wanes, the girl becomes anxious and begins to hold onto him. The more she clings, the more he withdraws.

If they emphasize companionship, common appreciations, the things they do together, they develop the capacity to be great friends and great companions. They call to the best in each other, traveling the roads of destiny together. Then they are one in heart and mind and soul, and their oneness in body will be a sacrament that will grow in beauty and meaning into the very sunset of their lives.

Thus they fulfill the capacity for the first great function of marriage. Monogamy is fundamental to the nature of man and is essential to his ultimate fulfillment, but, like the Kingdom of God, its blessings can be achieved only when the great requirements are met.

When we look through the pages of history, we see some great marriages which, like the great persons involved, are brilliant lights in the sky of human experience.

There are not many in the Bible. Adam and Eve may have had a good relationship in some respects, but something was wrong, for their first-born murdered his younger brother. Abraham and Sarah may have found a good life, but something went wrong, for Sarah was unable to conceive. Why? Once in Egypt, Abraham denied that she was his wife and that night she was forced into untold indignities. This could have been such a deep hurt that it blocked her capacity to conceive. In her later life she heard God tell Abraham she was to conceive and she laughed. Could this mean that now she had finally got beyond the hurt, even though perhaps her laughter sprang from her doubt?

Isaac and Rebecca missed the real thing, for recall that the mother preferred her second-born and influenced him to deceive his father.

Jacob and Rachel may have known a good marriage, though he had ten sons by Rachel's sister, Leah. Jacob deceived his father and was in turn deceived by his father-in-law and by the sons born to the woman he didn't love.

One of the great marriages was of Ruth and Boaz. A new quality of love characterized by tenderness, mutual respect, and companionship may have come into the world through them. Their son was Obed, the father of Jesse, the grandfather of David, and an ancestor of Jesus.

The great marriage in the Bible was that of Mary and Joseph, for unto them Jesus was born. Mary was a supreme mother. Though older than his wife, Joseph must have been a good husband, for he was a wonderful father. Why? Because, when Jesus chose a name for God, He called Him Father.

When we look across the pages of history we see examples of great loves, such as the relationship between Robert and Elizabeth Barrett Browning, one of the greatest in history. How exquisite is the interpretation of love in Mrs. Browning's poem:

> How do I love thee? Let me count the ways.
> I love thee to the depth and breadth and height
> My soul can reach. . . .
> I love thee to the level of every day's
> Most quiet need, by sun and candle-light.
> I love thee freely, as men strive for Right;
> I love thee purely, as men turn from Praise. . . .
> —I love thee with the breath,
> Smiles, tears, of all my life!—and if God choose,
> I shall but love thee better after death.[1]

As I think of the great number of families I know well, there are those who stayed together because they found the misery of marriage less painful than the misery of separation. But there are hundreds of couples who have found a meaningful relationship, joining with their children in finding the high meanings that are known by persons who travel the five roads we have taken in these pages.

There is a third group, small but eloquent, who are seeking and finding real excellence; these are they who are achieving wholeness of life as individuals, lovers, parents, workers, churchmen, and citizens of the free world. The persons blessed with this greater union are finding what millions seek but miss. Together they find a special dimension of power, of meaning, of understanding, of transforming in influence, that is almost startlingly unique. They bring a quality of perception, of creativity, of life-giving power, of whole-making love, that leaves its impact on all they do and on all the persons to whom they relate. In the deepest sense they become "radar stars." They are those in whom the divine incentive is expressed and fulfilled in the quality of life which can come only in marriage.

We must say, however, that in marriages that fall short, often there is one of the couple who becomes a "radar star." Also, there are those to whom marriage does not come, but who become married to a cause of a high purpose and who father and mother hundreds orphaned by the loss of parents or by parents who failed them. While they find a gratifying equivalent, perhaps in their hearts they know that there is a union which, if fully known, would give their lives fuller meaning.

A second function of marriage is to provide the environment for children. The significance of conception we have already pondered in Chapter 2. For two persons to experience a relationship which offers an opportunity for continuous growth is wonderful. For them to join in bringing a new life into the world approaches the divine. Their love bears fruit. And now they have something they can love together. If their love is real, this must deepen their relationship.

A third function of marriage is to provide the environment in which lives can grow from conception along the paths we have named. It is in the bosom of the family that personality is formed and nourished. If the nourishment is rich, the person becomes of the quality the world needs and yearns for.

This leads us to a consideration of the relationships between parents and children. Everything we hold dear depends on our children, actually. Every baby that is born represents a second chance for the world.

## *PARENTS AND CHILDREN*

First, parents need to have a good relationship with each other before they can form healthy relationships with their children. If this is the case, it usually follows that:

1. They can set limits in a way that enables the child later to set his own limits. But these limits must be set out of their understanding of the child—not of their own needs and ambitions.

Firmly-set limits make for secure children. The overly permissive parent's love for his child is too often based on a need to be needed and loved. It is not a gratuitous outpouring tempered by a healthy sense of responsibility and self-respect. And so the parent gives in to the child rather than exercise the self-discipline required to set standards. The end-result is a creature of impulse, the gratification of which brings restlessness and self-loathing rather than satisfaction. Often the world will forbid such a person to do just what he wants in all instances, and he won't be able to understand or adjust.

2. They will respect the feelings of the child, who, in turn, will feel free to express his feelings to them.

One night one of my grandsons stayed with us. I was told that at 9:30 he was to go to bed. As the zero hour approached, I said, "Time for bed."

"I don't want to go to bed," he whimpered.

"I'm sorry if you don't," I told him, at the same time taking firm hold of his hand and leading him upstairs, "but this is the way it has to be."

"I hate you!" he cried.

Now, suppose I'd slapped him across the mouth? What would I have accomplished? I might have persuaded him to be more polite in the future, but I also would have removed myself permanently from his confidence. Instead I said. "Go ahead and hate me if you want to, but right now you're going to bed."

By this time we were in the bedroom. Now he changed his tactics. "I won't be mad at you anymore if you'll read to me, Pap," he said ingratiatingly.

"I have no need to be forgiven by you," I said. "The simple fact is you're going to bed."

He actually seemed to be pleased with my attitude. "Okay, Pap," he said finally. "I'll go to bed. I love you," he added.

"I understand how you felt," I said. "I will read to you for a bit."

The next morning he crawled into bed with me and demanded, "Pap, why am I short?"

He wanted to share with me something that concerned him deeply. This was wonderful. The night before I had done two important things: I had set limits, and I had respected his feelings. Now, in the morning, he trusted me with his feelings.

3. When parents are still growing in their life of love together, they will respect the rights of their children. Children do have rights, you know. But so do parents. The trouble is that it's not always easy to strike a happy balance among all these rights. Let me illustrate.

Here's a family with three boys and a dog. The dog turned surly and began to chase people who passed the house. One day he bit a neighbor boy in the leg.

That night, during their family meeting at bedtime, they talked over what they should do. It seemed that they had no choice. They would have to get rid of the dog. The eldest got very worked-up. "If Jet goes, I go," he declared.

And so he did. He packed his bag, and at nine o'clock he started off with Jet. His parents put on a good face as he left and then sat down to wait.

Within an hour the boy was home. "I went so far," he sighed. "I went so very far away, and I'm so tired."

His parents hugged him and loved him. "It's so good to have you back, son," they said. "We missed you."

As they helped him undress and take a bath, he said, "You

know, Jet is growing up? He really is. I think maybe we should get him a job."

From the mouths of babes, they say. Actually, this was a very good idea. Jet liked to chase people and nip them—why couldn't it be cows? Mother and Dad put their heads together, and within a week Jet joined the army of the employed. He became cow-fetcher for a farmer sixty miles from town.

A few weeks after delivering Jet, the family went to visit. The farmer had nothing but praise for the dog. Jet himself seemed glad to be called upon, but showed no signs of wanting to be taken home.

A few more weeks passed, and the information came to them that Jet was about to become a father. When the blessed events arrived, the family went again to visit. The puppies were cute, but Jet's fatherhood had transformed him. Or maybe it was time. In any case, he growled ferociously at one and all. "Why does he growl at *us?*" the children wanted to know.

"I guess he's left our home for good," Mother explained.

The children have not asked to return since.

Now, consider how easy it would have been for those parents to have mishandled that situation. Instead, a solution came about in which the children themselves participated, one which made it possible for them ultimately to renounce their pet of their own volition. No unfeeling authority handed down a decision or solution from on high. It ended up happily for everybody involved—even Jet. Had it happened differently, the children might have carried the scars through life. As it was, they were administered a comparatively painless lesson in the always difficult course of growing up.

All of this implies that parents should be good listeners—not only to what their children say, but what they're trying to say. If parents will only listen, and listen carefully, they will know where their children are. And with this knowledge, they can help them move forward: steadily—gradually—painfully, sometimes; but *forward!*

4. Parents who are doing right by their children in the sense

we mean use the mistakes of their children as occasions for *teaching*, rather than excuses for ventilating their own bottled-up feelings. They never call their children *bad;* they explain why whatever it was went wrong. Sometimes no explanation is necessary. The lesson is obvious. Particularly where the example has been set, and is reliable, and the standards have been consistent—the occasions for preaching diminish. This is not to say that wrong should be whitewashed. Quite the contrary. But judgments must never be punitive. If they have to be made at all, they must be wrought in compassion.

The healthy parent gives *himself* the right to make mistakes as well as his children. If he can do this, it will follow that he can be easier on the youngsters. His judgments thus can be practical rather than moral. And if they are practical, they will usually be moral.

5. Finally, parents should attend sufficiently to their spiritual life so that their children will come to know God before they can pronounce His name. If they live in a fellowship of love, it will be easy for them to come to know God. Indeed, it will be inevitable. For God *is* love.

But there are formalities along the way that will help. The table blessing is a ritual that can instill an understanding of man's relationship to God from earliest childhood. As the children grow old enough, they can share in the table blessing. On holidays, or days of some special significance to the family, different forms can be used that will enhance the meaning of the occasion and give the children a real sense of participation. A candle might be lighted, for instance, with a child doing the honors should his performance be appropriate to the occasion.

Another important ritual is that of bedtime prayer. This can be expanded to include a pre-bedtime worship fellowship for the entire family. Children are naturals for such an observance, since they are proverbial fugitives from bedtime. With the youngest baby there can be a ritual of worship that develops a sense of security. As he grows and learns to understand language, bedtime can become a time to bring together the experiences of the day, to share, and to come to a real sense of God's presence through Scripture, prayer, and such symbols as a worship center.

I recall one family who followed this plan. Now their children are grown, but when they are together in the summer, the grandchildren look forward to the bedtime fellowship and worship. After they're asleep, the parents and grandparents linger together late into the night, for the closeness developed in childhood reaches into their adult lives.

It is important to expose children to great music and to great spiritual classics other than the Bible. In each home there should be at least one picture with a spiritual message. On the wall of one home "The Presence" hung for years. The parents never knew until the children were grown how great was the influence of that picture on them.

A worship center can mean much in a home. It can be located almost anywhere the family chooses. One family I know has one in their study. On a shelf in the bookcase is a cross, a statue of St. Francis, a piece of driftwood shaped liked praying hands, and two short candles. When I was there recently, I found a boy standing before it. He is in the seventh grade and studying advanced math. I went over and stood beside him. "I'd like to be alone, if you don't mind," he said apologetically. "I have sort of a personal problem to take up."

I retired willingly, thinking, "What a wonderful thing to have in a home!"

## CONCLUSION

With all the openness prevailing today in discussions of sex, many married couples remain confused about it. Even in their weddedness, many feel that when they have intercourse they are giving in to the flesh, that they are lowering themselves. This is not true at all. If they love each other, if they are one in mind and spirit, their bodies seek union in a sacramental sense. So when they become one, flesh and spirit are one. It is like unto the experience of the bread and the cup. This attitude does not reduce desire; it frees it and gives it the high meaning God intends. In the right relationship, love-making never becomes old; it never loses its joy and thrill; the glory of it reaches into the sunset of life. Thus it is not only God's way of bringing new life into the world, but of deepening the spiritual union that makes two truly one.

Thus their relationship can be an eloquent example to their children. Questions can be answered suited to capacity, and children can grow up understanding their feelings and believing in them.

The members of the family need to do meaningful things together. They become a family through the sharing of common experiences. No matter what his work is, each husband and father will plan time to be with his wife and family. How much he is with them is not as important as how fully he gives himself when he is there. What does it profit him if he gain the whole world and lose them?

So the family talk things over. They are a fellowship. They plan times to be together. If they begin when the children are little, it will be natural. They share joys. They pool wisdom. They take trips, even if they are short and for week-ends only. They plan for the family; they plan for individuals. They work out budgets together. They build a philosophy of life. They seek to be citizens of the whole world. The concerns of each are the concerns of all; the joys and victories of each are the common pleasure of all. Yet while they are close, each is an individual in his own right, with his own views; his life is his own to live.

# CHAPTER 20.  THE SCHOOL

Since I am not what might be called an "educator," I hope that this chapter will not seem presumptuous. However, I do have some background in the field of education that may lend credence to the few points I wish to make in these pages. I taught in a country school one year, was a high school principal three years, and acted as superintendent of a vocational school for one year before going into my present field of work.

During my years as a youth leader and my twenty-five years of service in our spiritual laboratory, I worked very closely with elementary and high schools. Each year I have spent time in a rural or small-town school and also in a city school. In the past three years I have had many experiences with student groups and have addressed faculties in all parts of the country, including the Hawaiian Islands.

Out of this background, I am led to offer a few suggestions as to how the school may be instrumental in developing whole-making relationships.

## THE SCHOOL HAS THE TIME

In an increasing number of school systems the educational process begins with five-year-olds and continues through the twelfth grade. From the earliest compulsory age to the latest, then, all children are in school. A little more than half of our young people graduate from high school.

The school not only has the children five days a week for the school term, but for many activities over the week-end. In many communities the school conducts a program through the summer in recreation, crafts, athletics, and other special courses.

Some school systems are now developing camps, where super-

226